American Husbands

American Husbands
and Other Alternatives

By
ALEXANDER BLACK

Essay Index Reprint Series

 BOOKS FOR LIBRARIES PRESS
FREEPORT, NEW YORK

STANDARD BOOK NUMBER:
8369-1021-4

LIBRARY OF CONGRESS CATALOG CARD NUMBER:
68-57305

PRINTED IN THE UNITED STATES OF AMERICA

To
CLELAND RUTHVEN AUSTIN

SOMETIMES, I have no doubt, a preface should be headed "Errata." But even if it is not used for apology, even if the happy liberties of our new era lift from the author the need simply to say grace before serving himself (while hoping that he will not prove to be tough), the alternative to a meek preface that hopes is not, of course, an impudent preface that assures or directs. The real occasion for a preface (aside from the decorative function) is that the writer needs the release of an irresponsible gesture. Should the writer be able to persuade himself that the thing does not matter, he may go on with it, being as casual as he can about the documents, and remaining ready to retort, should any one find dissonance in the diversity of his offering, that this is just what enlightenment has learned to pardon, if not to welcome, in the moods of an individual. He may insist that only the preface is deliberate, that all the rest simply happened. This will not be more than rhetorically right, but it will make a sort of point. And having picked up his manuscript, he may add, for example, that he is indebted to Harper's, Century and the Bookman for permission to include certain essential (and highly significant) elements of the array.

CONTENTS

American Husbands

AMERICAN HUSBANDS

PROBABLY the American husband is a mistake. Yet before deciding to change him, even before listening to his own theories of extenuation, it will be fair and profitable to glance at the testimony. It is possible that in offering a plea of guilty he may have been too impulsive. On the other hand, it may be that his plea was intended merely as an insult to the panel of feminine jurors.

We can not look for a disinterested witness, but one from a distance must have the appearance of not being entangled in the quarrel—that is to say, in the American quarrel.

The sort of thing visitors to the United States say about us—to us—naturally falls into a formula. These visitors may come with a benevolent expectation or with a grouch; they may be going away happily reassured or in a state of bitter disenchantment; they may be hoping on in the face of the awful evidence or be

3

nursing a verified exasperation. Such diversities do not greatly affect certain standardized comments. If the visitor is polite there is the impulse to say what is expected. Challenge works to the same end. Since what we expect also is standardized, we get what is coming to us.

Male visitors may vary prodigiously in endowment and in disposition, but they all say that American women are wonderful. Some of them say it shyly, and some slyly. Others speak with an emotional ardor that suggests an elated passion for discovery. As a device to please this is invariably successful. We know it has to happen. Yet we expect no real man to say less. Male visitors anywhere on the visitable earth have been saying something of the kind since times older than interviewing, in answer to instincts older than gallantry. The man who emerges from the jungles of Uganda will tell you about tribal belles whose beauty and charm are simply astounding. It is all part of a biological imperative. A man who did not think the women were a mitigation probably should not be trusted. Of course, if he goes too far, and peoples a South Sea island with dazzling and enterprising flappers, the misguided multitude of responsive men who scurry across the Pacific to find the paradise full of fat old women will have an opinion of their own.

4

American Husbands

The woman visitor to the United States, in this as in other particulars, is more complicated, not, perhaps, in her actual reactions, but in her expressions. Chiefly because women are less perfectly adjusted to formulæ, they often disappoint those who look for the established word. Plainly, they do not always feel that American women are wonderful, and they are hampered by a delicacy. A man-made tradition permits an exuberant "To the ladies!" But it is another matter to ask women to eulogize the men. This isn't done. Aside from the traditional awkwardness is the question of discipline. In the crisis the woman visitor points impressively to the American husband. It is to be gathered that one may speak of husbands without seeming to expound men. There is, too, often an effect of implying that only the husbandly relation makes the traits of men of any importance.

It was a woman who first remarked that men differ but that husbands are all alike, and women from abroad who have studied us have doubtless made their analyses upon some such theory. Women who have been married several times admit sharpness of variation between one husband and another. Naturally, nearness emphasizes difference. The remote moves into a classification. Thus, the American husband has been noted by those to whom he is exotic as a specific

5

appearance, as a kind of creature with special color and markings. Feminine commentators who began by speaking vaguely and appreciatively as guests, have frequently gone away to analyze and discriminate. From these cases we learn that the American husband can be not only bewildering but incredible. No European training seems to help very much in any effort to understand him. He blends traits that do not belong together. He violates ethnological grammar. He is absurdly docile, yet fearfully self-centered. Professionally he has imagination. Domestically his mind is blankly plastic. Publicly he is a pusher. Privately he does what he is told to do. He is submissive without gallantry. He never really worships. He only offers sacrifice. Even his brutality, when it happens, lacks the grand style that belongs with a technique ripened under classical conditions. No woman with a cave-man complex can hope to do anything with him.

Such analyses have not prevented the foreign critic from saying that she does not blame the American woman. The assumption appears to have been that any sane woman who cared to marry at all would take advantage of such opportunities. Unless all signs were delusive, it was receiving odds in the wager to get an American husband if one could be had, and was known to be true to type. To be true to type he would, of

American Husbands

course, have money. No man without money can prove
that he is indulgent. Moreover, the foreign impression that the American husband talks about nothing
but business implies that, in all fairness, a wife who
has to hear inordinately about money-getting should
profit proportionately. The listener is worthy of her
hire.

Probably it is a waste of time to linger over foreign
opinion, as much of a waste of time as eliciting it in
the manner of so many of our interviewers. We can
not prevent foreigners from writing about us, and we
can not seem to prevent ourselves from reading the
things they write. It may be true that social relativities ought to be measured from a distance. The notion
would sound plausible. But where are the experts?
Mr. Einstein's brief excursion into social relativities
seemed to be no better than any one else's. Quite like
any one else, Mr. Einstein extolled American women.
The movies have not needed to reduce this particular
dictum to a diagram. He is credited, too, with declar-
ing that American men are lapdogs of the women.
This is doubtless full of meaning and suggests greater
complexity of explanation. Assuming that it is meant
to be a rebuke, or an admonition, it lacks something
that we ought to look for from a scientist; or perhaps
the thing it lacks is something that we ought *not* to

look for from a scientist. I am not sure. Meanwhile I have the feeling that distance has not helped Mr. Einstein. In spoofing us he does not rise above the ordinary.

If we had in America a sociological Einstein, one who could fix for the common mind the parallels, curves, tangents and nuances of matrimony, who could show how and why so many of our social straight lines are not straight at all, the part temperamental refraction plays in the incidences of the social system, and so on, we should be able to turn more hopefully to the study of a fascinating and painful problem. Of course, there is no such person. He would be married or not married, and either situation must disqualify him. Evidently it is ordained that we should grope.

The sheer drama of groping after new grounds for complaint against marriage is one of the marked excitements of American life. Rebels are ever busy searching for a novel uncomfortableness. They are slow to see that all marriages are marriages of convenience, that marriage is, indeed, the Great Convenience and still awaits the invention of something just as good; that other conveniences must, of necessity, come into competition with it. For example, the husband who agrees cordially that his wife shall keep her maiden name, knows that in the conflict of the two

8

conveniences the greater will conquer the lesser. Except in the case of professional expediency, wherein only the stupidest reactionary resents the keeping by the woman of the name she calls her very own (though it includes her father's), the acceptance of the conforming "Mr. and Mrs." is quite likely to win use as the easiest way out of a basically awkward situation. To be simply "& Co." in the social firm is, in view of woman's actual equalities, a paradox. The point is, that it is a convenient paradox. As usual, that is determinative. The social unit idea may label the man as nominally the head of the firm, but sentiment should be able to get some satisfaction from the fact that "Co." in business is often the real boss. Obliterating her name is but one of the things a woman chooses to do in the interest of coherence for the family, and the name she obliterates is, after all, simply the name of another husband for whom her mother made the same sacrifice of identity.

It is as the titular head of the family that the American husband comes in for the sharpest criticism. Both foreign and domestic critics are, on occasion, glib in asserting that he does not properly act the part. We are told that the foreign husband, good or bad as an individual, holds his place; that foreign children may be brought up without a fear of God but not without a fear of father; that foreign wives always know who goes first, whose tastes determine the dinner and the ventilation, who leads the conversation, whose slippers must be warmed, whose nap must not be disturbed.

Of course, these generalizations about the foreign husband would look funny enough in Europe, but they serve as a handle for the switch that is laid on the American husband. There is at times an effect of stirring the American husband to assert himself, not only in his own interest, but in furtherance of the unifying reactions, as if the happiest women and children would be those who wore wound stripes. The joke is, evidently, to pretend that the American husband is a sweet person, enamored of a cynical beatitude: Blessed are the meek for they shall be married. Yet the divorce-court records seem to show not only that he can be abstractly unsatisfactory, but that he can specifically fail in meekness. Evidently the lapdog notion has something wrong with it. There may be something wrong with the whole theory of his self-effacing simplicity.

I recall the voice rising out of a group where a new play was being discussed—a new play to which one did not take one's aunt. "Girls!—it is so gloriously *male!*" The earlier and more confident Freudians would have known quite how to classify the sign.

American Husbands

Vaulting the intervening verbiage we may note the protest that there is no country in the world among whose women a glorious maleness is more unpopular. However, it will not suffice to deduce over much from the premise of the American woman's passion for pictured virility. Other regions of the earth reflect the same interest. Theories of an escape or of a decadence have discrepancies. But maleness as a fact certainly suffers sharp scrutiny in the United States. It would be saddening to believe that American women, wives among them, after decades of devotion to the high task of taming the American man, were now influenced to the point of doubt by the frequent European criticism that the American man, while absurdly "nice," is a wholly inferior lover. Nothing could be more pathetic than a picture of the American wife as seized by a remorseful horror in contemplation of what she had done to him. To conjure such a picture one would need a splendid faculty for illusion. What every woman knows is that a woman improves a man, so that if he ever is convicted of not being a Perfect Lover it will become plain that he never had the gift.

To be sure, we ought to remember, even in a parenthetical recognition of foreign comment, that foreign impressions of the American husband really began to happen in Europe and outlying parts. There is no probability that any visitor to these shores ever came without at least a slight prejudice germinated on the other side. The American husband has been too visible abroad to have escaped being seen. And if he has been seen he has suffered. Nothing could be less impressive than an American husband trailing after an American wife who is frantically occupied in checking up on all the things she will be asked about when she gets back. He would be brazen enough to admit that he hadn't seen the Sistine Madonna, or even the Venus of Melos. But she would know better. It will not do to say that she also may have excited prejudice in Europe, to cite the fact that, for instance, there have been a thousand allusions to her shrillness. Any resentment arising from her unabashed audibility would only serve to make his obscuration the more pitiful. In Europe as elsewhere a too patient boredom is often mistaken for meekness. When the American man is bored, as with teas, or study clubs, or picture galleries, and chooses not to make a row, the effect is stultifying and unseemly, though it may appear to him better than a row. He wants the price he pays for not doing or knowing the things he doesn't want to do or know to be a quiet price. He pays, and the picture of him paying is not imposing. I have witnessed his gentle bewilderment in the wake of a wife who was after Art, as patient with her culture as with her hat, perhaps knowing that both were quite new; and I could believe that no European was likely to guess him—not in the Uffizi. Perhaps Einstein had watched him, too.

A sociological Einstein would clear the ground by showing, as he might without effort, that, as most of the complaints registered against marriage should really be registered against life, so most of the complaints against the American husband do not properly lodge against his Americanness, or even against his husbandly relation. He may have helped to invent democracy, but he is not wholly to blame for its inevitable effects upon wives and children as well as upon husbands. The American habit of trying to keep a jump ahead of trouble may, in fact, often account for a way the American husband has of relinquishing, and relinquishing with an honest cordiality of assent, that which must surely be taken away from him. Now that even the Turk has seen a light, it would be grossly out of character for the married male in the United States to brace himself against the new spirit. He shows no disposition to do anything of the kind. To recognize both children and wives as persons can involve heroic renunciations. The degree of the heroism must depend upon the inherited luggage of the individual, and upon the nimbleness of his sense of humor.

Yet children who regard the old man as a good sport are probably better fun than children who pretend to be obliterated when the ogre stalks in. The traditional master of the house was a stark figure. He may have been logical, but he was lonesome. He was indispensable to novels and plays. His way of cutting off the son, and of banging the door on the disobedient daughter, especially when it had begun to snow, facilitated plots enormously. He is still good for a sob if it can be arranged so that the mother will do no more than look heartbroken in the crisis. Somebody really should hit him with a chair. This would cure him, but it would spoil the story.

It can not be denied that the American husband is a great spoiler of heavy plots. He is better in comedies of exasperation. Recognizing a wife as a person leads straight toward those little annoyances that loom large in the critical effort to keep the old outlines. Take the matter of his babbling about business. Romance has always revolted against the idea, and it has been shown again and again that keeping romance is essential. Nobody pretends that as between telling the truth about business and telling lies about love there is any real choice. But there ought to be no such alternative. A husband should have a better instinct for the things a fully recognized person will find interesting. He should himself have more than one interest. Even golf clubs are not a wholly satisfying variation. A proper education would enlarge his chances of being a good dinner companion. Like many another, I am acutely sorry that the American husband does not read more, or read better. Leaving the book-reading to the wife and worrying along on a radio culture lead to his ruthless elimination as a person. He ends by becoming only "Him."

A husband esthetically inferior must ever be, as George Eliot said about a difference of taste in jokes, a strain on the affections. The habit of not noticing a wife's clothes, even when the trait is in no way aggravated by a habit of noticing other women's clothes, has forced many a husband to give disproportionate and less appreciated praise to spiritual qualities of the wearer. Every man knows that homage to a gown, as a gown, gives a woman more satisfaction than a masterpiece of compliment which includes the woman herself. Few husbands show any aptitude for utilizing this knowledge. Few avoid the blunder of being flippant about clothes. It does not matter that a husband's vaudeville jest, "That's a pretty dress you nearly have on," is used to conceal a real chagrin over the physical display. Such sarcasms are a bad investment.

Married romance is, indeed, as fragile as ever. The essential subtleties can not be made light of. Yet a study of the nice points is precisely the sort of thing for which the American husband has no flair. Naturally, he shows to the least advantage where chance has mated him with a fearfully feminine woman, as, for instance, with one of those women who shed handkerchiefs, gloves, and other objects on all occasions. He may have become accustomed to her shedding responsibilities. It is the fragmentary thing, that jerks him into awkward action, toward which he feels most savage. There are women whose facility in dropping reaches the dimensions of a gift. Usually they are women who become greatly preoccupied with interior and theoretically invisible, but piercingly evident, garments that often need to be tucked down, but that more often need to be pulled up, especially at the shoulders, to which, by design or neglect, they are always imperfectly adjusted. Hands upon which are imposed so many obligations of search and seizure inevitably lose control of other things, and a man invested, permanently or by chance, with the responsibility of picking up has to have a good deal of jumping-jack agility. He may, while possessing other talents in plenty, be inferior in this one, and come to recognize the fact. Or he may be resentful from the start. A handkerchief or a fan retrieved for the fourth or fifth time in one evening may begin to look damnable, and the woman owner to look like a disturber of the peace; in which case the perfect poetry of relationship must suffer a bruise.

The European husband probably knows what to do with a wife who is a shedder. He knows the sign language of the dropped thing when the dropping is an art, but he knows, too, that this art has not a promising place between husband and wife. The European husband may be versed in the theory that sustained romance implies sustained coquetry, but all husbands will be found to agree that a woman must choose, if not the kind of coquetry a man understands, at least the kind he likes. Naturally, the same compulsion applies to a man's technique. A husband with the wrong gestures of gallantry can be a severer trial than one without any. Brute simplicity is seldom a mere bore. Women have died of it, but never in hysterics.

Although husbands hate to be told that being married is an art, they are, on the other hand, almost as much irritated at being reminded by a practical wife that it is a business. A man who wants to loll amid domestic comforts can be unreasonably impatient over the details of the effort by which these comforts are produced. He is willing to know, domestically, what time it is, but he doesn't wish to see or hear the wheels go round. This is the hazard of married continuity—the behind-the-scenes contact, the sustained attritions of intimacy by which we are sometimes on the verge of verifying William James' discovery that you can't have anything without having too much of it.

The American husband and wife can make a good public impression. At their best they publish well. The husband, as a husband, is seldom a strutter. The wife may lead rather too obviously on occasion, but unless the husband follows meekly instead of with the tolerant pride that is more characteristic, her effect of being advance agent and spokesman for the firm is never likely to be resented.

Yet no success in public can greatly lighten those natural difficulties of private adjustment which have no nationality. A husband is more than a spectacle. Unless he is mated to a fashionable wife who is always somewhere else, he must be lived with. Few meet the test. American theories of equality and frankness serve to make the test harder. It is committing a triteness to remark that large considerations, such as Mr. Howells was examining when he decided that after so many centuries of effort man is imperfectly monogamous, are less poignantly present with the average woman's nerves than those minor but vital phases of the human animal that build the sum of Him. When she hears him sleep or clear his throat, or winces at sight of the soup in his mustache; when she sees his lips distorted by a reeking black cigar, watches the ashes drop into the rugs, and steels herself to tolerate the stale odor of tobacco; when she counts the crises of collar buttons and shaving, the tensions incidental to the eight-fifteen, the fumblings and forgetfulness of the man who is (by his own account) a miracle of efficiency in his business; when she detects in his complaint against circumstances the effect of a complaint against her—as if *she* had neglected to wind his watch; when she realizes his readiness to promote her to the office of unsalaried valet and to accept all her talents as natural features of feminine endowment, she may excusably doubt whether she is as much "spoiled" as Europe thinks she is.

The accusation that he spoils his woman is quaintly congenial to the American man. To feel lavish is to feel a kind of sultanic superiority. A man may bask in such emotions. He may feel as flattered as a German who is accused of having an iron hand. Traditionalists have no trouble in showing, to their own satisfaction, that American women really are spoiled, as much spoiled as the children. The American husband and father rises to say, "I did it," perhaps with a good deal of complacence. Whether he goes on to explain that it is simply tradition that has received the blight will depend largely upon his interest in the subject. In any event, he is likely to be unrepentant. Smashed traditions can not be put together again, and if it is too late to reintroduce the ogre rôle, it is too late to argue about it. If it is necessary to assume responsibility to justify his abdications, it is comforting to pretend that he prefers the results. He listens to the catalogue of the American wife's sins. He has his own special catalogue of her peculiarities. He is foolishly annoyed, it may be, by profoundly little things. He may notice that at six paces the design in her veil looks like a hideous birthmark. He may wish that she had the sense to wear glasses when she needs them, that she had at least one pocket for her train ticket, or that she wouldn't eye him while he goes through twenty-one pockets after his own. He may review her sins, like the shrill talking, and her follies, like the clumsy make-up, and call it a day. Since it is all part of his very thorough job of spoiling her, who shall presume to complain? He doesn't know anything about art, but he knows what he likes.

In his crude way the American husband is an idealist. It would deeply please him if he might be accused of filling the bill—if She happened to admit or contend that he measured up.

American Husbands

I can remember being shocked and charmed by an American wife's analysis of the reasons why, to attain a perfected sublimation, she should have three husbands, three concurrent husbands.* Under such an arrangement the Business Husband who went forth would have a splendid freedom of action. He could concentrate on office efficiency, production, distribution, road or mail-order sales, the entertainment of buyers, late-in-the-evening club conferences, out-of-town conventions, and the showy wives of purchasing agents. With his activities fully accounted for under an intensive specialization, there would be no need to decode his answers to any connubial questionnaire. Where he had been, what he had done or had neg· lected, would involve no questions, would be of no more than academic importance so long as the returns were satisfactory. Any incidental uproar would mean simply more money. With his mind free to forget the furnace, he could start off in the morning on high gear, radiant with productive expectations. That the house roof had begun to leak would be to him a triviality concerning only the Handy Husband. The Handy

---

*At the time of the first publication of this paper in *Harpers* for August, 1923, the innocent pleasantry of the three husbands occasioned some ingenius comments, and at least one high spirited vaudeville sketch by Jack Lait. A certain more recent discussion has seemed to omit the formality of quotation, a circumstance which would have no importance save for this later appearance of the original escapade.

21

Husband would be selected solely with regard to his versatility in tinkering. He would know all about hollyhocks and manure, laundry traps, hot-water bags, can openers, garbage pails, screw drivers, picture-frame wire, camphor chests, and Yale locks. He would know how to stop windows from rattling, subdue the obstinacy of doors, turn mattresses, wire a lamp, air a rug, mend a doll, or rationalize a vacuum cleaner. For him the eight-fifteen would not exist. He would always have time. He would not have to synchronize with commerce. Nothing that he forgot would have to be explained by the insistent whisperings of a business conscience. His handy mind could expand. His imagination, kindled by a joyous freedom to putter, could rove through the uttermost recesses of house and yard, find pure poetry in potato knives, and attain a kind of religious fervor in polishing the piano. He could reach that destination dreamed of by every liberal soul, unhampered individual expression. It would be a happiness to a wife, when not otherwise occupied, to observe his processes, to see him, dressed in becoming overalls, ecstatically concentrated, like an artist, in training up the peas, and to know that for every triumph of his genius she was the inspiration.

Then there would be, of course, the Lover Husband, a glorified Nice Man, tall, but not too tall, romantic, pleasantly emotional and, at times, perhaps even tempestuous, but a moderate smoker, meticulous in the matter of clothes, though capable of a certain spirited casualness in wearing them. He would swear just enough to give him a manly effect, but his profanity would be refined as became a man who looked well in church. He would be a good dancer, bright at bridge, with the correct voice for reading aloud, a cheerful taste in ties, and a discerning interest in dinners. He would be moderately witty and a noiseless sleeper. Being freed of the sordid distractions of the Business Husband, and having no diversity of duties such as must fall to the Handy Husband, he would always be right there. He would not want to read the financial page. He would not be ruined as a listener by any habit of wondering whether that noise meant trouble with the kitchen boiler again. He would, in fact, be no more subject to bedeviling distractions than either of the other husbands. Each, like an endowed specialist, would be, and could afford to be, winged by high purpose. In ensemble they would assure the perfect home. Automatically, the wife also would become perfect.

To the theory which I have here translated rather freely, the American husband makes an obvious response. With characteristic confidence he asks why he shouldn't be a candidate for the position of composite, why he shouldn't aspire to be a beautiful blend, to win the honors of all. Optimism could go no further. I can fancy the wistful compassion of the Average Wife; her disenchantment, skeptically tolerant, with something of the maternal, as of one who has suffered all and chooses to go on. It would strike her as so like his cheek, this aspiration to be all things to one woman. It would remind her that a male creature can be ridiculous yet be capable at times of a certain magnificence; that one may smile at the graveside of Respect.

Yes, it is utterly true that the American wife respects the husband less than husbands used to be respected. But she seems, for some reason, really to like him more. And if this became the common impression how would it affect the future of marriage? Is it possible that the familiar hesitation of young women will be inverted by their brothers? Will the young man, stilled before the great debate, weighing cautiously his individualistic impulses, then turning to appraise the absorbing enterprise of marriage, be heard asking himself: "Shall I stay single, or go in for a career?"

The Young Person

THE YOUNG PERSON

SOCIAL critics who give the effect of scowling out of a petticoated past at the antics of a one-piece civilization are likely to be heard prophesying a fearful reaction. There have been, indeed, threats of a kind of Fascist feminism one of the results of which would be a reversion no less momentous than the coming back of the Young Person.

The Young Person of tradition had a Cheek to which no one, on any account, must bring the Blush of Shame. The restraints imposed upon human society by the Young Person's cheek were enormously significant. This cheek became a kind of barometer, the reading of which regulated not only sociology but the arts; so that when, in the course of time, it seemed to be discovered that the cheek had ceased to be a surface and had begun to be a quality, that impudence had taken the place of demureness, social sentiment was staggered. Apparently, the shattering of standards from this cause alone inflicted one of the sharpest pangs of the War.

The Young Person

Of course, the Young Person had begun to fade long before the War. The image of that traditional cheek might be held with fanatical desperation, but its owner had ceased to be vivid. She was, it is to be noted, older than the Victorian. It has been the fashion to paint Victoria as her goddess. But she was born long before Jane Austen. Perhaps she reached the height of her influence in the middle of the nineteenth century, when she not only furnished Victorian literature with an inexhaustible theme but marked impressively a certain boundary. Her wistfulness threatened like a barbed barrier. It was what Darwin must do to her that made him an ogre. It was a theory about her which divided authors into sheep and goats. A literature was made for her. There began to be magazines that were her very own. It was about a hundred years ago that she was reading *A Manual of Elegant Recreations, Exercises and Pursuits*. She was not permitted to read honest-to-goodness novels. Sweet substitutes were provided. She nibbled these things, like chocolates, with an adorable resignation. She was sharply separated from her brothers. Coming-outs were invented. When she was finished in some school she went forth into society. When she was married she went forth into life. She was to know nothing at all real until her husband chose to tell her. He was to decide what it was good for her to know. Knowing anything more was unwomanly. In fact, the system was beautifully devised to make her a hypocrite.

And she was a hypocrite. There was a pictorial charm and other attractions in her hypocrisy. Her father, having encouraged her to be a winsome liar, liked the effect. Her husband liked it. Even her sons learned or pretended to like it. But all this time she was a human being, living in the midst of other human beings. She had the job of living, and the job of knowing could not be diagrammed quite so easily as the system managers assumed. She might look like the theory on the outside, but inside she was, as the phrase runs, something else again. As a man-made idea she was tremendously over-sexed—the stressing of a male conception of contrast in general and docility in particular. The thing she was asked to be belonged as completely to a strictly male idealization as did the harem. So much for the theory, the plan. As a fact, she was simply the female of the species, basically a human being, incidentally female, and her natural instincts, whatever might be done about their expression, could not be thwarted completely by any esthetic formula or counter sex prejudice.

The pretense could not last forever. The conspiracy between maleness on the one hand, and older

29

women representing social interests on the other, began
to crumble, and the Young Person, meanwhile, refused
to stay young enough or ignorant enough to give the
plot any plausibility. The discovery that women were
persons was followed by the discovery that even children were persons. A newer education introduced notions of human development which made it hard to
hold in place the arbitrary rituals and schedules of a
venerable system. Stodginess took fright. To this
state of mind the beginning of the present century was
the beginning of the end. If youth lost its innocence
and began eating of the tree of knowledge before it
had received permission to have a digestion, the gate
of the garden must soon close against it. If youth
went to the bad, what hope was there for civilization?

As usual, when civilization crumbled the world
found something just as good. Viewing with alarm
continued to be popular. The changing of the Young
Person was indicated as appalling proof that the future held no hope. Manners were decaying. Youth
that no longer cringed was mischievously defacing the
temple. Education actually began to truckle instead
of to mold. The modern girls' college became as different from the Victorian seminary as—well, as the
modern girdle is different from the Victorian corset.
Awful talk about evolution made it impossible to think

of "finishing" a girl. Conservatism realized with chagrin that the world was frightfully unfinished, and that the girl, like the rest of it, was simply on her way. Girls went into business at about the time their brothers did. It was not feasible to keep on being a Young Person in a rush hour. You couldn't be wistfully withdrawn in daily sight of a dictating boss with a thick neck. A youth that mixed in affairs, that read newspapers, that began to get acquainted with the world it was living in could no longer be segregated. The sophistry of a special knowledge for a special age required conditions which had been brushed away. The truth is that youth always knew what it was old enough to find out rather than what it was old enough to be told, and the changed situation consisted mostly in the coming of something that was a little closer to honesty. Honesty meant acknowledged privilege, acknowledged responsibility. A society that set about abolishing classes was bound to find that the young had been made a class, and that this classification was as untenable as any other. The young were young, just as the ignorant were ignorant or the poor were poor; but the democratization of life, if it was a good theory, must mean that if poverty, for example, were not to be an imposed condition, neither was youth to be penalized for its youngness. The inherent penalties of being young, like the inherent penalties of being old, can not be done away with. What democracy asked was that penalties should not be invented, that it was a useless and hazardous hardship to keep on asking youth to deny knowing the things it knew, to avert its head, to withhold its hands, to perpetuate hypocrisies about its "place." When woman stopped having a "place," so did her daughter.

The change spoiled an old picture that was supposed to be beautiful. The picture was beautiful when it was beautiful. Also it was hideous when it was hideous. Girlhood in that old picture could be, and by many a revelation often was, a maddening slavery. More frequently it merely dulled. Always it tended to stultify. Emancipation brought the usual bewilderments. The strong who had habitually wiggled through were not hurt by the change. The weak had to find their feet in freer going. The new picture showed much confusion.

And then came the War, fear, hate, hysteria, and the flapper. Youth behaved like the rest of the world. It would have been comforting to have had youth ignore the delirium, to have had it wait, close to the gate like good children, until the excitement was over. Unfortunately, the excitement lasted a long time and the factor of example had its effect. Youth made a free translation of mature conduct. Generally, the translation was quite faithful to the original. The young girls' clothes mimicked the old girls' clothes. When so many social safeguards came tumbling down, it would have been asking a good deal to demand that youth keep its fences carefully mended.

The spectacle of the flapper has been painful as a picture and as a symptom. We did not need the cartoonist to tell us that the flapper could be funny. Street giggles anticipated the print. Yet she was less funny than the prototypes. Painted nakedness can take on a genuinely comic cast only in the mature. In the young this funniness carries a disturbing note. The frightening effect of the typical flapper has depended upon the age of the spectator, upon the acuteness of any sense of implication; or, let us say, upon the sense of humor. How much the flapper has represented the legitimate joy of youth, how much a devastating loss of restraint, how much pure neurasthenia has been open to all sorts of opinion, and there has been plenty of opinion.

It is to be remarked that lightened domestic discipline for the young inevitably places a special tax upon the instincts of daughters. The son is always more definitely under the discipline of circumstances. In the matter of manners, for example, the son is constantly subject to the stress of an operative criticism. He can be knocked down. His queer hat can be knocked off. A trace of loudness or preciosity in his clothes is sure to elicit more than a guffaw. He is reminded that a mere mannerism may block his business progress. He is constantly in the presence of codes.

Outside the home the discipline of the girl is much less closely codified. Fashion is an excitement rather than a discipline. The sanction of fashion is fashion. The boy who starts in to sow his wild clothes is not only brought up with a round turn somewhere, but is roughly or otherwise reminded that man does not live by clothes alone. The wherewithal for clothes puts a tax on ingenuity which both sexes must meet; the disparity appears in the young man's need to buy entertainment for Her.

There is the story of the young man who asked the city girl whether he might call on a certain evening. In a homelier era girls studied various arts of entertainment applicable to times when men called. They made fudge or played the piano. There was recognition of a balanced interchange by which she presided over a home evening and he provided adventure at the county fair or town hall. We do not know precisely what was in this young man's mind when he strode forth, whether his expectations were flagrantly

The Young Person

sentimental or quite without dream elements of detail. We know only that he was misled. "When I got there," he said, *"she had her hat on."*

Before we measure the calamity to the young man who was, as this story went, forced to spend four weeks' savings to meet the presumptions arising from the fact that she had her hat on, we should remind ourselves that this girl had no parlor or piano. She slept in a flat called home, but she lived largely in the great open spaces of a city. Her notion of an evening was going somewhere, and in these great open spaces going somewhere means money. Thus entertainment became a responsibility belonging solely to him. Her contribution was her company. He contributed *his* company, but this, in common practise, is to be estimated as of lesser value since he must add the money to balance the bargain. Under these circumstances the morality of the young woman's position is full of subtleties. I can not make it seem less than cruel to deduce that, if her company is worth more than his, her company must by these terms be sold to him. It is always fascinating to watch her shrug out of the dilemma, as if the dilemma were nothing of the kind; and the niceties of the argument (I mean the theoretical argument, for no one really *does* argue about it) are still further complicated by the fact that the young man, discover-

35

ing that she must be bought, likes to buy her when he happens to have the money.

Among young men to whom money considerations are no embarrassment, going somewhere received lively encouragement. Home and its arts went out of date. The domestic phonograph gave a certain impetus to impromptus in dancing, but the motor horn furnished a more potent music. Doing anything without a car became equivalent to doing nothing at all. Social life ceased to mean assembly. Chiefly it chugged. When we are through with all other analysis, the automobile will remain the most conspicuous of explanations for the transformation of social forms. All human functions for the enterprising fell into the classification of things you might do while the car waited. So far as the young girl was concerned, the duenna had long since disappeared. The chaperon, after becoming a non-intrusive joke, was finally forgotten. The automobile took her place as the third party.

For the sentimental the flapper era was, indeed, a fearful disenchantment. The one thing that era seemed particularly to repudiate was being sentimental. So much emotion had been wasted on a mere war that a great many springs went dry. There were signs of a wish to accentuate rebuke of all sentimentalism about feminine modesty. I fancy that as an era it was less deceitful than some of its lamented predecessors. Humanity, young and old, may have been finding various avenues of escape. We were reminded, for example, that sensuality came in with clothes. There was no difficulty, on these lines, in arguing for fewer concealments—this era specialized in exposure. The spiritual parallels are equally tenable. If inhibitions make for hypocrisy, and we hate hypocrisy, why have inhibitions? If complexes make trouble, why generate complexes in the sensitive years by saying "Don't"? Nothing could be easier than such a plan of escape. There is something wrong with the plan. One can not linger over it long without realizing that it leaves out something. The thing it leaves out is the thing the hustling American business man most insistently looks for in his business: it leaves out the vital element of results, that total of the sum which the most ambitiously liberal of us has to estimate at last.

There are two especially interesting implications to a "don't" either in life or in art. One is the implication that the expert may counsel the novice. The other is the implication that control serves expression. Conservatism, wringing its hands, asks frantically: if we may not be taught and must not take command of our instincts, what invention is to supply the place of these expedients?

The Young Person

Of course, there is no such crisis. The social disturbance started by the poison of the War had not the dignity of a revolution. It was not even a disease. It was only a paroxysm. It was, in the first place, the flowering of social liberty with which American theory had let itself experiment. Moreover, the flowering was forced, as when you put hot water on the stem of a cut plant. The War fevered all relationships. It hurried a cycle.

I have (as you will have noticed) ventured to speak of the flapper in the past tense. Technically she went out some time ago. The easily pleased who can get comfort out of the pendulum image are sure that the swing to safety has set in. Perhaps something less stultifying than automatic reaction has really happened. Of itself, a lowered temperature is no proof of returning wisdom. Yet betting on American sanity is supposed to be betting on a sure thing, and it may be a patriotic duty always to be getting ready for the entry of an undebatable common sense, even of common sense about the young.

Assuming that a change has set in, how will it be manifested in the young? What is to be the new attitude toward the young, and what is to be the attitude of the new young? It would be absurd to suppose that any social stocktaking could be likely to result in the reapplying of ancient formulas of authority. Parenthood might try putting on the lid again, but no disposition to do so would meet the case. The spirit of youth has escaped from the old container. It must be bargained with. A change which the young did not "get" on its own account would not be one from which we ought to look for sure returns. The notion of a bargaining would have been shocking to ancient disciplinarians, yet something of the kind, however cloaked, has always been going on. To-day's difference is created not only by changed theories of possible pressure but by a franker feeling about personal choice.

Meanwhile we are bound to note that the connotations of conduct have more than an external effect. There was a day when, if a woman's hairpins slipped and her locks tumbled, she was as if helplessly compromised. The girl who chanced to be kissed at least began to be "undone." We may gather that thereupon she often exhibited an attitude of mind that left any subsequent happenings to appear as mere detail. The modern girl is not to be gathered in the momentum of such traditions. By the simple expedient of denying the implications she stands free again. Definitions of conduct must continually be rewritten. When Saul of Tarsus admonished against braided hair he spoke by signs. If you braided your hair you were likely to be marked as a certain sort of woman. If Paul had returned in the Victorian era he would have had to revise his code, for pigtails had become the symbol of adolescent innocence. Returning to-day with a revised prejudice Paul, confronted by a much exposed girl with carmine on her lips, would be quick to say, here is a woman of the streets or a chorus person en route from one theater to another. The chances against his rightness would be ten thousand to one. A Jane Austen without fresh enlightenment would be in the same situation. Standardized translations are quite useless. To make the young understand that social pressure goes by translations is a huge anxiety to guardians. To make guardians understand that a change in the original implies a change in the translation is the eternal trial of the young.

Manners are, indeed, not a dead language and each age reserves the right to new accents and to new codes of definition. Quoting a gesture as meaning this or that can be as obsolescent as citing Chaucer. The female of the species once required seven or eight petticoats to establish a certain idea. There is no magic in establishing the same idea with no petticoats at all. But stodginess hates to change symbols. It can not get away from the notion that chastity, for example, is promised or repudiated by fixed indications.

The Young Person

This is not to deny that chastity itself has a symbolical phase, and that making new terms with biology is more momentous than cheating a social dictionary. A youth that takes charge of its own game and that says it knows what it is about may be nearer a practical prudence than one that moved in the dark of an ignorance. Because it is youth, and because it asks to be liberated from the formulas of that collective discretion we call morality, it will face special hazards. But the new liberalism seems likely to win some advantages in doing away with false formulas, though truisms will survive the formulas, despite the corrupt mature who flatter folly in order to appear young.

We have to live before we know how. There seems to be no way of rearranging that. And this fact keeps on giving a dramatic twist to all decisions. At the moment there is the effect of a world of young and old returning sullenly, sheepishly, whimsically, defiantly, to truisms. The fascination of the different, the sheer refreshment of getting away from old stuff, are explanation enough for many a fling. It is the yardstick or the commandment, the fact or force of which can not be denied, that present a constant temptation to run. These explain quite as fully the comfort of coming back home. Even a wise radicalism is apt to forget its daily dependence on the basic. Soon or late every excursionist into delirium must return to the real things—to beauty, babies, character, and other fundamentals. I suspect that youth, like age, is capable of discovering that the north star is quite where it used to be.

The flapper herself, it is indicated, found out that flapperism didn't pay. This is not to endow her with any special sagacity. I do not mean that she really saw what had been happening, that she had a glimmering of either the tragedy or the comedy of herself. I mean that in the end she felt the pressure which is the definite regulator of human conduct—the social pressure which has so many ways of making itself felt, in a school yard as well as in a jail yard, a ballroom, or a legislature. The young may never, on their own account, discover that theories of conduct were not arbitrarily invented, but they are quick to get the results of their own experiments, not in logic but in response. The exhilaration of chucking tradition, of being ingeniously shameless—which we have seen in artistic conduct as well as in social conduct—may never be rebuked by the discovery that tradition is simply the accumulated results of previous experiments, and that a sense of these results is what we call culture, but it can not escape the discovery that it really needs and has looked for response. When response fails, when our own class, applying the closest pressure, shows apathy or disgust, the game palls.

Certain traditions are very important to the young girl. Effects of charm or of mystery represent a significant asset not to be overlooked by self-interest. She may abandon mystery, as in the dressing of her body or her mind, and diminish the chance that some one will marry her out of curiosity; but giving up charm is another matter. She may act on a wrong theory, yet the human stuff she is made of precludes the likelihood that she will ever consciously give up her lure. Ordinary feminine shrewdness was bound to listen to the accusation that her lure had faded, that she might be picturesque, that she might be a good diversion, but that she had begun to look like a poor investment. In the end she was sure to find that being regarded as a good investment was at the very front of her interests.

Not her interests alone have whispered to the young girl. She does not escape having at least rudimentary ideals, a fine or frivolous sense of destination—it is in youth that ideals are born if they are to be born. And ideals finally draw her glance to the compass. The social compass tells her that, though outward signs be subject to revision, though the language of life be in a state of flow and formation, no one has budged the simple fundamentals. Allowing for eccentricity and high spirits and plain frailty, we still acknowledge, even though it be from some highly literalized angle, the theory of a gentleman, still uncover reverently before that feminine equivalent from whom the washlady has stolen the name. Unless theory or practise can modify our sentiment of admiration for a certain sort of man and a certain sort of woman, it is unlikely that youth will ever lose a sense of these images. So long as this admiration is acknowledged we are not destitute of a clear-shining incentive to young adventurers.

The Young Person's descendant, the exuberant freshman to whom the flapper has become a sophomore, enters a situation with all the old perils intact but in which there is less noise and an admonitory wreckage that will hardly escape her attention. In her freedom to see and to hear she will know that some things have not paid. She will find fundamental things thrown into a certain relief by the subsidence of the clamor and the clearing away of the dust. She will raise a merry dust of her own with her car. It may be that she will like the radio better than reading. That will depend much upon her family's state of development. She will not be a knitter—certainly she is not by way of being a *good* knitter—and she will never, like her remote ancestor, aspire to be pale. Neither will she be demure or *dévote*.   She comes into a nervous, hustling, self-conscious world, a world of reforms and efficiency and dotted lines, that talks slogans in its sleep, and no one will expect her to sit by the ingle with her hands in her lap.   She is likely to live where there isn't any ingle, and where it is necessary to invent some other symbol suggesting that one may stay at home; she may, indeed, be further prophecy of that day when each individual's home will be under his hat.   It will give her a good laugh to recall the days when girls carried their hats in their hands and ate lip paste with their meals.   She will have the newcomer's advantage of not missing the things which in an earlier era she would have thought she needed.   She will see through the cheap pose of being bored.   It will not amuse her to be *blasé*.   She inherits a jazz called classical, a slightly lessened responsibility as to dreams, a complete map of sex, and a routine knowledge that the brontosaurus would be a living factor to-day if they had taken out its tonsils.   She will not know for a long time that each era seems feverish to the survivors of the one before. She will take herself and the United States, if not outlying parts, for granted, and have a privilege profounder than her ancestors' of making her own mistakes.

Whatever these mistakes may be, she will make

them in an enormously illuminated world. If she is differently foolish she will find herself under a spotlight. If she is humanly sensible she will be printed and pictured anyway to please those who insist that everybody must be either young or scandalous. She will have heard that wedding notices should be put in the amusement column. Cynicisms about the sacred will be too commonplace either to shock or to amuse her. The noise of them will be old to her before she begins to think deeply, since she will have heard everything. Not to be able really to "come out" because she has never been in, will mean that nothing can strike her suddenly. She will be no more subject to social surprise than a girl brought up on a farm would be open to astonishment about orchards or cattle. Not being able to be wistful about weddings, she may come a shade nearer to belief in the theory that staying married is simply being a good sport, even if she reserves the right to quarrel with the rules committee.

Her world will tell her that it has been disenchanted. Sour preserves will not interest gatherers of fresh fruit. And she will see spring as they may see it who do not remember too many autumns, see it with the penetrating, wonder-working glance of youth. In her ignorance she will make her share of blunders, and by the divinely precious good fortune of not knowing that certain great things can't be done, will go ahead and do them.

Our grandmothers, said Anatole France, were romantic. The young of to-day are quite of the same opinion, save that this time the judgment applies to the period in which brother Anatole sat in meditation upon *his* past. Evidently one can not be so "hard-boiled" as not to seem soft to those who have passed through years of a higher temperature. Yet we have been promised a period of romanticism. Who knows that the notion may not appeal to the flapper's successor, and that she may not usher it in? Certainly, it can not happen without her connivance. She may attain great concessions. Who knows that some one may not contrive, for example, to make gentle speech fashionable, and that she may not, after hearing the shrillest voices in the world, herself become low-voiced? It would be a fearful radicalism, but at this juncture romanticism would be radical and, after all, the flapper's successor may hate the noise as much as the rest of us do. Who will venture to predict that, though she may refuse to be a hypocrite and will know too much to be enslaved by any awe, she may not, indeed, find high satisfactions in the sheer art of being a young girl—in rehabilitating an art by whose vicissitudes all other arts are delayed in coming back?

The Hokum Saga

THE HOKUM SAGA

SLANG, outcast cousin of Poetry, black sheep, nimblest of all the court fools of civilization, continues to be a merry trouble-maker. He has no repressions or remorses. No dignity awes him. When he clowns in you may expect a crash somewhere. To the guardians of verbal crockery he is more terrible than an army of bannered syllables. Without shame, yet without malice, in the midst, for example, of a delicately perfected analytical arrangement, he can bawl out, "Bunk!"

No use asking where he found it. The care-takers in the museum of language know that the mischief is done. The word is coarse, as coarse as "mob" was to Dean Swift. People who like to be gentle with the erring, particularly with erring ideas, shrink before the ultimate word. With them it is as when we say to children, "Don't point!" And when the ultimate word is not only ruthless but vulgar, with no proper parents, the case is at its worst. There is too an emphasized annoyance when the intruder is native. The home scamp is a special responsibility.

The Hokum Saga

At the moment we need not be concerned about this word bunk's ancestry or previous servitudes. It is quite probable that, as usual, it does not come of good people on either side. Maybe a Buncombe County or a bit of Canadian French started the trouble. Then there is the sporting strain, with banca, banco, the banco steerer, the bunco steerer, buncoed and so on. Let the professional genealogists make the chart. The fact remains that bunk has grown up, has been nominated and is openly a candidate for election. Examination shows a capacity for the essential gestures,—*bunk, bunking, bunked,* not to speak of the interesting derivations *debunk,* and *debunking,* to which forcible effect have been given by W. E. Woodward, the stalwart author of "Bunk." There is no mystery of meaning, and there is the thud that comforts the instinct to chastise. We can not escape the impression of impact. It does not belong among the solemn fighting words but rather among the mischievous missiles. It can be the custard pie in the face of cant or crookedness.

To the native critic of native frailty the word becomes precious in the processes of ridicule, by way of indicating that as a people we prefer to be bunked, with the implication that the essential industry might find another people or another time of which the same thing were not true. The tawdry fact is that what we

call bunk is elemental. History bristles with signs of
it. The instinct to bunk runs with the willingness if
not the craving to be bunked. The Barnums of business, of politics and of art know that the trait is in-
tegral, and act accordingly. Less subject to general
suspicion is bunk's handmaiden, *hokum.*

Hokum often travels simply as the adjective to
bunk's noun. Bunk would blunder fearfully without
his helper. Hokum can carry the anesthetic. An audience, a whole people, can be stupefied by hokum until
a major operation of bunking is painlessly complete.
By the aid of even a crude application of hokum, a
fanatic group can be kept for a long time in a state of
ecstatic delusion. Inevitably the fumes affect the operator. Primary intentions are forgotten. Hokum for
hokum's sake often leads to a delirium of drivel, a kind
of hasheesh orgy of sentimentalism, in which the entrance of intelligence would seem like a brutality.

If there might be a war without bunk—a wild hypothesis—it is inconceivable that without the inebriat-
ing help of patriotic hokum humanity should be able
to create new occasion for the spectacle of five hundred blinded soldiers marching to L'Etoile. Sinister
self-interest can make a religion of bunk, but it needs
a ritual. Hokum casts the spell. In the end the historian, especially, of course, if he is native, finds it

more glamourous to ignore the bunk and record the hokum. The historian may catch a full glimpse of the leer of bunk. There is more of picturesqueness in hokum sobbing, "My Country!"

Bunk, then, is simply the element of fraud, big or little. Hokum is used to facilitate the technique of seduction. Naturally, hokum provides the accepted dope of diplomacy. Political palaver used hokum before it used clothes. Even the solemnest statesmanship inevitably learns that logic is lean fare and hokum a good relish. Give them the fixings. Dress the picture. Be prodigal with God's-country hillsides and hearth-stones and vine-covered porches and twilights, or in desperation, an aurora borealis. In a cloak of hokum, gallantry hides the bunk of sex deceit or contempt. Women are supposed to have a precocious instinct for identifying bunk in any disguise, yet to adore hokum. Better hokum than a hiatus. Real sentiment is notoriously hard to get at or out, since discernment or response may exist without the faculty for saying or showing, and may find occasion to clutch at a tattered symbol. Many an honest blunderer has been saved by a bromide. Women have a way of implying that the real thing is pretty much a theory and that it is more practical to take masculine hokum not as a deceit but as a deference.

54

The Hokum Saga

Thus has been developed the specialist in hokum, in the something-just-as-good of civilization. To acquire votes without hokum would be to work a miracle. Constituencies know nothing about art, but they know what they like. Imagine a Daniel Webster trying to "get a hand" without hokum! It would be harder to fancy Ingersoll, who was a performer fertile in devices for engendering emotional receptivity. Burke, sparing as he could be, knew as well as Gladstone, or Disraeli, or any other spellbinder that a noise like a speech implied, at some point, tremors of sentimentality. Huxley could lay the bricks of logic without emotional mortar, but he did not have soap-box obligations.

The specialist begins where oratory with a conscience or science with a preoccupation leaves off. If hokum gets the "hand," if something mushy calls quicker attention and holds longer memory than something of straightforward integrity, why not have a larger proportion of it? Since every orator finds his hokum, above all elements, getting itself quoted, why not build on hokum and slather disingenuous ornament over the whole structure? For filling the hall, for all forms of popular appeal, for trick propaganda, for "selling talk," the practical necromancer assures us that imitation sentiment, *i. e.,* hokum, is, to the profane, more satisfactory than the original. It is true that original sentiment calls for an original response. And the world is tired. The familiar is easier to assimilate. The old joke, not too intricately reclothed, the stolen garment of an old song, the emotionalized platitude, like patriotism that is a quotation rather than a feeling, all save effort and bring corresponding comfort to those who need to be saved.

Thus the specialist looks upon hokum as we have formed the habit of looking upon legal tender, not as intrinsically equivalent to the gold of true sentiment, but as if, convertible without loss, it were an imperative convenience.

The strongest argument for hokum as advanced by the specialist is not that people prefer to be deceived, for they would deny that hokum is a deception, but that your average man, and especially your average woman, prefers old stuff. The game of the specialist is that of standardizing average reactions and deliberately working the mechanism that sets these reactions in motion. Pulpits are, of course, prolific in this sin. Many a preacher is to be classed among the specialists. When theatrical stop-pullers say "sure fire" they mean that not only a type of thing but a definite device always wins a laugh or a tear. Tears themselves are all but invincible. A woman with a facility in synthetic tears can be a hokum artist of high rank. The crippled beggar, playing upon the emotion of pity, can earn five thousand a year by a gesture that belongs to the essence of hokum. He is a true pragmatist, like the skilled manager of tear ducts, and refines his art until it operates with a beautiful certainty. He would be capable of arguing that he is not guilty of bunk. He does not deceive. He has the infirmity, you have the pity weakness. His guilt is solely that of being an artist—an artist who prefers his art to real work.

The professional patriot operates on the same principle. You need to be assured that you love your country. He needs the money. His use of hokum completes the equation. The working basis is quite as good when the hokum artist trades on the theory that you love God or your mother. If you love God, any expedient for tapping the emotion starts with a noble major premise. Your tenderness toward motherhood, since it is an indispensable morality, should be encouraged by exercise. You may escape natural occasion. Thus devised occasions give to Mother-hokum a perpetual respectability. Also Mother-hokum assures profit, for it belongs to the category of "sure fire."

All the arts have a theoretical horror of hokum. The literary artist with his passionate avoidance of second-hand words, is too often caught with an inner-circle hokum of his own. While his critical police are raiding books or plays for illicit popular hokum he can have a still in his own cellar. His decoctions are for the elect, for his own kind. Free-verse hokum, for example, was among the flagrant diversions of the late lamented rebellion. The get-literary-quick people were soon drunken with the discovery. To these there was a great thrill in being free of laborious literature. No more hard thinking or meticulous labor. Leave out capital letters, scrap the punctuation, find a few forbidden words, sufficiently puzzling to the profane, and the trick is done.

At this juncture it is the fashion to hate quotations, chiefly, I have no doubt, because these are a reminder that something, that anything, has been done before. Blessed are the different for they shall inherit attention. The difference-obsession explains both the comic and the morbid in resulting art as in resulting conduct. Fundamental things must be punished for the trait of being trite. Spring and space, conflict and humor, friendship, jealousy, bread and babies are old stuff and their sin must not go unnoticed. A dread of the familiar can neither face nor escape them all. Even an ambitious distortion of them ends somewhere in hysteria.

Sometimes it seems that the fun-makers are most secure. Being disrespectful to the equator is part of the game of having fun with the immutable. Fool's Hill is at least an eminence, to be considered with the other High Places of profound tradition. However, it is not art's frivolity but its fear that saddens us. Nothing could be more pitiful than art with a case of nerves, shrinking in an alert horror of hokum. It is not alone in being neurotic about things that are not done. In fact it behaves very much like the general. The prosperity of books that inform you about which fork, indicates plainly the prevalence of a nervous social instinct that dreads to be X when it comes to the telling of what is wrong with this picture. Art often seems quite as eager not to forget form, not to get its spiritual spoons on the wrong side, not to serve anything that has ever been eaten by the vulgar.

If all of us are, in some degree, and in one way or another, hokum swallowers, it is hard to see how we can comfort the hokum hunters. Fundamentals have a way of staying put. We have not been able to get away from motherhood, for example. Ten thousand silly mother songs do not obliterate the fact that babies are basic. Neither literary lapdogs nor any actual menagerie of poodles can change our bromidic biology. Synthesis may yet do something about it. There are people who have hopes. Yet even an era of new science in which women should escape an enslaving function, if only to affront the arrogance of men, would still find the baby an imperative, and if there were babies there would have to be mothering. Even institutional mothering, when it had inspired sentiment in somebody, would lead logically to new hokum—to new trading on human emotions.

Should war be done away with, the blow at bunk would, it must be admitted, result in an enormous loss to the hokum industry. Orators, factories devoted to making tin soldiers for village squares, headstone and floral designers, bonus propagandists, specialists in hating foreigners, home-market school-book historians and memorial poets would all feel the loss. Yet no one will pretend to claim that the hokum instinct is unlikely to find new escapes, or, on the other hand, that quite reasonable expressions will cease to give the offense of having happened before.

If we go on laughing at jokes that have an archetype, and crying over situations devised sordidly to take advantage of our better natures, what promise can we offer to the sensitive artists who insist that every chuckle and every sob shall have a strictly original incitement? And what can be done about the incorrigible tautologies of Nature? The habit we call Nature has never been impressed with the sinfulness of doing anything again. No wonder radical art is always asking a divorce from her on the ground of incompatibility. Certainly Nature is poor company for bored souls. The same old clothes, the same old technique—what shameless encouragement to hokum-hawkers! The stodgy can point to her as eternally classic. People who live in an exquisite fear that something with a seemingly innocent newness will prove guilty of having been done, are doomed to repeated pains. We must go on having weather, wanderlust, fashions, books, bandits, indigestion and governments. If we are to have some one to talk to and to govern, to wear and handle and stare at our inventions, we must go on having children. Old stuff is always with us. And hokum knows it.

Hokum is, then, in a fair way to an uninterrupted prosperity. If we have good times it will invent ways of orchestrating our sighs of content. If we have hard times it will weep with us, for it can be a wonderful Sarey Gamp. When we are lazy it will lure us into justifications. When we are hurried, when we must do our reading running, when we haven't time to live, it lives for us for a very little down and easy payments. It is always ready to favor a mood for sleep. In its dream forms it is not less fantastically versatile. We see a face we seem always to have known. Now it is the comfortable protagonist of platitude. Now, mimicking the traditional small voice, nourished on canned conscience, it is a miraculous pinch-hitter for our so-called better self. Through the wonder-working of hokum we may, indeed, get the equivalent of real intellectual experience, as by radio, without compelling our mind to leave its lounge, without even forcing upon ourselves the strain of being wide awake. We are privileged to feel the envelopment of a standardized world and to nod assent when, in the matter of affections or bereavements, efficiency mutters, Say it with hokum. Possibly it is true that we have permitted life to become so complicated and exhausting that we may no longer hope to live in the original, and that a Hokum Age is essential to salvation. Let him that is without hokum cast the first complaint.

One Night Stands

ONE NIGHT STANDS

THEATRICAL people have a special cynicism in the matter of one-night engagements. Readers and lecturers also will betray to you bitter reasons of their own. I remember an hour on a Texas train with F. Marion Crawford when the talk took up these little miseries and made drama of them. All platform people meet on a level here—they all must keep on moving. Each repugnance has an indivdual shading. Thus Conan Doyle, on his first tour, hated above everything the heat of Pullmans and hotels (he tried going without underclothes). But the common adversity of being perpetually moved on cemented a fraternal contempt. Mark Twain cussed about it in the grand style and rejoiced in the time when he could pay Major Pond a hundred dollars a year to say No for him. I had the feeling that he might like to have the letters read, "No, damn you!" Bill Nye and James Whitcomb Riley could give a twist to their partner experiences not easily to be paralleled. Will Carleton, Hopkinson Smith and George W. Cable brought nothing to the platform

65

that seemed to me quite so good as their private legends of the road. In General Lew Wallace there was a dignity of resentment. Max O'Rell moved like a hardened rounder. One did not worry about men with a real circus talent, as with the Fat Contributor, but gentle spirits, like James Lane Allen, helped give one a fury against the hardships. Matthew Arnold and Herbert Spencer had the way smoothed by personal management. So had Henry Ward Beecher. The fate of personal managers is another story. Ibañez and other temperaments of a later day probably have not presented worse problems than those faced bravely by care-takers for temperaments that preceded them. Traditionally, the extreme case is that of a male lecturer with a prima donna disposition. I survive as one of the victims who, after the manager had diagrammed the tour, "rolled their own."

Nothing is more vivid to a survivor than the picturesqueness of "opera-houses." The Tremont Temples and Carnegie Halls recede into a standardized frame. To ask for the opera-house and find it up a stair over the butcher's, was a special strain on the imagination. In the ghastly gray of daylight one of these places had the look of a slattern in curl papers. The gallery, carpeted with peanut shells, was likely to be particularly reminiscent of barn-storming leg shows and impressed a mere "reader" with a sense of inadequate saltiness. One looked forward to the evening as to an ordeal in which he would be found wanting. It was possible to fancy platoons of the audience walking out, noisily (crunching through the peanut shells), and himself as taking the stipulated check from the committee with a sheepish acknowledgment of having been impudently expensive. The best consolation you found at five P. M. was the thought that what these people really should have hired was a juggler.

Then came the surprise of the evening, when the bright audience filled every seat and perhaps strained the standing spaces. This was the recurring miracle. One stepped off a train amid a shabby group of buildings, looked across the stretches of winter country with one or two visible homes, faced the chagrin of the opera-house, and wondered how more than, say, sixteen people could be assembled, even by force. Perhaps in the interval one picked up the weekly township newspaper and chuckled desperately over the irony on page five: "What Society is Doing." Allowing for a few houses at the limit of the horizon, the most abandoned imagination could not conjure a real audience, certainly not a two-hundred-dollar audience. Yet the impossible happened. At eight o'clock Paris hats sprang out of the drab landscape. With lights going the opera-house had a better complexion. It actually glittered. And the people, in a modish mass, showed a cheerful and challenging alertness. Where they came from was now an obliterated problem. They were there, as to an opera first night, expectant, important. The best you might have with you no longer seemed any too good.

In a Kentucky town my performance was to be in the court-house, the judge's bench being removed to establish the proportions of a platform. The forward seats were filled by an impressive company of girls from a near-by college; there was the effect, in the audience, of a social event. The performer's waiting place, in which he abided the summons from the chairman of the committee, turned out to be the jury room. Under broad daylight this cavern might not have looked so much like a chamber of horrors. Actually it was a squarish room with walls of white plaster, or plaster that once had been white. As discernible in a flickering yellow light a nervous one-nighter saw it as a place of purgatorial pause, needlessly depressing to one who was soon to be called upon for gaiety. As so much psychology it became shocking. Yet I found occasion to remember that it was, basically, not a star's room at all. Its severity might be quite correct for juries. A juror does not need distraction, but only credulity and concentration. The walls told me, presently, that he had needed, also, private means of outcry. Over every inch of the walls reachable by the hand were scattered chirographic writings. Numberless juries in pain had sought by the humble pencil to relieve the itch of exasperation. Here the sufferer was solemn or diagrammatic. There he leered or babbled as at the brink of delirium. A specialist might have built a book with photographs of this arena. As a visualization of the human mind it was cyclopedic.

Over near a window, in a script one might have pretended to recognize as a linear sarcasm, I read: "What an annoying thing it is to have eleven contrary men on a jury!"

Immediately underneath, in restricted space, yet with a John Hancock vigor that shouldered its way, came the inevitable yet somehow refreshing rejoinder: "What an annoying thing it is to have one damned fool on a jury!"

Could more than these two sentiments be needed to set up a social philosophy? Isn't everything there? Are not all possible questions as to art, censorship, morals, religion, and even diet, fully answered, for all time, by this apocalyptic apposition?

Once, when I was on tour with a stereopticon show (at that time I should have been insulted to have the thing so flippantly described) I came to a certain town in the South in company with my operator, a hardened one-nighter like myself. There was a line-up of hotel porters at the station. The biggest and brownest of the rush line clutched our bags as if he had been sent to do it, and, this being one of the towns in which we knew no hotel names, we followed meekly at his heels. We were too tired and hungry to wonder about our destination. The striding giant swung round a near corner, and in the middle of the block turned into a sullen place that seemed filled with chairs, all empty. A fearful emptiness affected the whole scene. Doubtless in the late afternoon it looked its worst. Our bags were set down in front of the desk, and our large guide, skirting the counter, pushed the register to our hands.

"You see, Tisdell," I whispered wearily, "he's the clerk, too."

When our signatures had been recorded the big fellow smote the bell powerfully. It sounded like a fire gong, and echoed vastly through the shadows. There was no response. Afterward I could understand that it was not a summons but only a gesture. Nevertheless there was a theoretical simulation of something resembling resentment, at the end of which the porter and clerk came back into the open and recaptured the bags. Our eyes said, "Also the bellhop!" and we climbed the longest single flight of stairs on the continent. Here were our quarters. Right over there was the dining-room. Supper when we were ready.

We came to the dining-room in a state of profound hunger. It was a dusty dining-room, with peeling varnished wall-paper and many flies. Since we had seen no human creature but the porter-clerk-bellhop, it was no surprise to find that we had the faded dignity of this cavern quite to ourselves. We waited lonesomely for some time and were gathering a large indignation when I discovered a bill of fare tucked under a cruet stand. This appeased us for a while. But we acquired a fresh petulance when nothing happened.

Then I caught sight of a line printed in brick red at the bottom of the menu. It said: "Impatience dries the blood more quickly than age or sorrow." To add philosophy to flies seemed too much.

"This sort of thing," I said to Tisdell, "never can be told. If I ever write it people will think it is more of my fiction. If you ever tell it, you not being addicted to fiction, they will simply think that you are a liar."

Tisdell was looking as if nothing, not even my pitiful condition, made any difference, when the swinging door at the end of the dining hall creaked startlingly and our man came in, wearing an apron. He was the waiter.

We glared at him as people glare who are past all jokes.

I pointed desperately to the first item on the bill of fare. The first thing might be quickest.

The face of the porter-clerk-bellhop-waiter underwent a twitch of chagrin.

"I'm sorry, boss," he said. "But I spoiled dat to-day."

He was the cook.

It did not matter that when we came down-stairs to go to the opera-house a venerable white man was at the clerk's desk, or that at breakfast a fat colored woman brought in the coffee. I had learned that one person could run a whole hotel if he wanted to.

In fact, the one-nighter, who is pictured by the lay mind as mingling enormously, as moving (in dress clothes) through shimmering scenes in which he is ever the central and significant figure, knows a tour by fearful details that make the advertised performance incidental. His actual meetings are with conductors, sleeping car porters, bus drivers, scene shifters, electricians, hotel clerks, waiters and committee chairmen—an interesting lot, humanly speaking, gifted in disillusion, and assuring excellent conversation. The committee chairman is not necessarily so cynical as the stage doorkeeper, but it often becomes his simple duty to remark upon the misfortune that your star course night should fall upon the same date as the wedding of the mayor's daughter, the D. A. R. reception and the Elks' ball. The implication is that if you find anybody in the seats you are a wonder worker. To make talk, the scene shifter tells you about the last picture-show when the light for the machine gave out. There is likely to be something wrong with the heating plant, especially in regions addicted to severe weather, so that the listeners may decide to keep on their wraps and to glare as if daring you to warm them. Under the best circumstances the radiators will make pistol-shot noises, each one killing a word—usually the key-word to a joke.

If the radiators pause for a space, there are always the coughers, who can orchestrate with the ingenuity of a claque. Staccato coughers, who kill words with a kind of stiletto thrust, are supplemented by people with large unctuous, reverberating coughs that bespeak a deep thoracic satisfaction. As between coughers and hysterics who laugh in the wrong places, actors and public speakers may differ in resentment. A long anger may manage to preserve a nice sense of discrimination as between the flavors of the two offenses, but the common longing is for chloroform.

In primitive opera-houses with visible stoves there was a tendency on the part of first comers to snuggle near the promised heat. Sometimes the stoves, if recklessly nourished, would become red-hot, glaring ominously in the twilight of the show, and necessitating the rearrangement of the audience. Until the snugglers had changed their seats I often found myself nervously anticipating the odor of roasting flesh. In one Vermont town the hall furnaces had collapsed altogether, with the thermometer at three above zero. I added overcoat, muffler and overshoes to the traditional regalia. These may have helped, but in forty-eight hours I was down with pneumonia.

Lyceum agents are, as they themselves will tell you, not always responsible for the whole horror of long "jumps." Changes of railway time-tables happen in the interval between the time of making an engagement and the time of filling it. Thus the night after Winston-Salem was to be Columbia, South Carolina. Theoretically this was conceivable. In a given August it might look within accomplishment for the following February. It was necessary only to drive, in the night, across country to a junction (whose name I have mercifully forgotten) in order to intercept a train that would intercept another train. The drive was long and icy. This was the South and, in a proper winter, it should not have been freezing weather. Moreover, at (say) two-thirty A. M., cold is never so disheartening as in the wrong place. We were driven by a very dark darky and a desperate expectation through miles that twisted and heaved, our heads wrapped together in a smelly blanket that shut out all but the cold. The junction station was open, but untenanted, unlighted and fireless. In the bleak dawn the essential train rumbled. But it sped by without stopping. At the appearance of a yawning station agent, whom we caught in the act of sinfully stealing oil-soaked waste from a freight wheel box to start the station fire, we learned of the changed time-table, and that there was no way of reaching Columbia until half-past ten at night.

Even an occupation that taught one never to give up found in this nothing better than a broken engagement, but when I had wired to the committee the details of the catastrophe, the cheery word was returned: "We shall welcome you at ten-thirty."

The word was not irony. It was not even indicative of a polite exasperation. That committee set to work with what one might have regarded as real gaiety to bridge an awkwardness of three hours. Ticket holders were informed, by a huge placard, that the show would not start until ten forty-five, and were admonished that they might have the intervening entertainment of attending the evening debates of the Legislature then in session. The legislators were told that they were not to be deprived, as they had supposed, of a star course opportunity. If they adjourned at ten-thirty all would be well. Also, the shopkeepers of the city were made aware that the curtain at the hall would not rise until after their closing time.

Of these resourceful expedients I was not aware during the last trying hours of the journey. An audience fidgeting since eight o'clock was the inevitable mental picture. The actual picture of Tisdell in the express wagon, with the gas-cylinders, going around that Columbia street corner on two wheels, remains vividly with me. At eleven o'clock the gallant southern audience in that hall faced me without a frown. The newspapers of the following day scarcely mentioned the lateness. And the chairman of the committee in handing me my fee, remarked, with a handsome cordiality, "Do you know, we made forty dollars extra by starting at eleven o'clock!"

Painting the Lily

PAINTING THE LILY

PRIMITIVE clowns, looking about for the face paint that would be the funniest, made many grotesque experiments, a few of which are preserved by art. It was found that various colors could make the features look soiled or sickly or fantastic, but that only one of the pigments could make them look completely absurd. This was white. And ranging the features for the one most vulnerable, the one most acutely sensitive to ridicule, they fixed upon the nose. Thus a white nose became an analogue of the ultimately comic.

If in the remote time of this discovery some seedy prophet had said to the clowns: "The day will come when the women of the world will seize your symbol and convert it to the uses of beautification. The whitened nose will become a fetish, a ritualistic sign, a supreme symbol of pulchritude," the clowns would have agreed, with a guffaw, that he was only a prophet.

And yet—

If in the same obscure era, when humanity was fumbling with the fundamentals, some philosopher had asked, "Which visible part of the body must, beyond all debate, be kept utterly clean?" the primitive pupil would have known enough to answer, "The lips." Ages later, after the invention of kissing and table manners, the answer would have been even more conscientiously emphatic.

And yet—

When paradoxes happen, instead of enjoying them or attacking them on their own account, most people seem to feel obligated to find a meaning for them in something military. Thus we are told that it took the Civil War to produce the hoop-skirt; that the Great War liberated the lip-stick. The theory looks like one of those ciphers by the aid of which you can read a secreted significance even in the "Help Wanted, Male" column. Of course there *is* a secreted significance, and this can serve to make the solution appear plausible. You may take anything that happens, and find that something else was happening at the same time. When Jonas Hanway carried the first umbrella seen in London, his radicalism was probably explained as a natural result of the Seven Years' War or as a reaction attributable to that impudent revolt of the American colonies. It might be shown that when umbrellas broke out in Persia centuries earlier, there was a parallel reason. The sculptors of the Takhi Jamshid,

Painting the Lily

judging by their designs, acknowledged the umbrella, and would have dismissed the matter with the usual theory; but they would not have suspected that China had umbrellas before that. Explaining things by wars may be a short-cut, but as a method of accounting, it is loose.

It is more subtle to dwell on the spiral of recurrence; to open any tomb and prove that the most ancient ancients practised this or that art or foolishness, if, indeed, they were not killed off by it. The Egyptians can be particularly annoying to people who have diagrammed a new neck-piece or a new dish-washer; and the Arabs (to ignore for the moment the exasperating Chinese) have taken pains to establish priority in an absurd number of devices, frivolous or wicked, which properly belonged not to the morning of civilization, but to the degenerate twilight. And the fact that the degenerate twilight persists in repeating itself is the eternal perplexity of the peevish.

Peevishness glares at the modern woman, and sees civilization dying again. It refuses to be comforted by proof of civilization's amazing gift for wriggling through, even by explicit testimony showing that civilization, when philosophically coffined, has repeatedly sat up, rubbed its eyes, and decided to take another chance at the great game. Either there is something wrong with the theory that if women go to the bad civilization is as good as dead, or else women have not gone to the bad when they were accused of doing it.

Probably the trouble comes from believing in signs. Astounding predictions have been based on signs that were as clear, in themselves, as coffins. The blunder came in decoding. Some signs may be like certain forms of pictorial art that do not mean anything, that are forbidden to mean anything. But admitting that all appearances have meanings, it is important, surely, to read them rightly or leave them alone. If much misery is to result from false deductions, if crazy conclusions can throw people into a panic, as if there were a war and we had on our hands a bunch of obstinate creatures who refused to kill anybody, it may be a duty to warn all and sundry, and especially violently reformatory or simply Klan-minded people, to keep away from signs altogether. Assuming that there can be degrees of danger, it is particularly important, in the interest of general happiness, to keep away from the reading of signs exhibited by women. Faith in civilization is too definitely vital, too necessary to common comfort, to make a false reading of the established barometer anything less than a calamity.

We may have needed the era we are living in, or living down, to test conclusively the whole theory of degeneration. People who view with alarm have never had so much to worry them. Eyes looking to women for a first and last warning of an impending smash have never been so sure that doom signaled. It has been pointed out, with a tricky effect of liberal review, that onlookers have been frightened before, but that always there was something left to go on. Women did this or that, yet held fast to the essentials. Just now everything has been swept away. With a gesture of horror, it is indicated that women smoke, drink and swear; that they speak without shame of things once reserved for whispers even by men; that they dress like dance-hall girls and paint like prostitutes; that the on-coming generation is already lost, since flappers and their successors, reared without modesty, reverence or religion, laugh in the face of authority and make no secret of regarding the whole theory of womanhood as hopelessly old stuff.

It might sound complacent to say that men critics of the time have shown less of desperation, have seemed less likely to turn into prophets of disaster, than women critics. For one thing, men are always more or less in a state of bewilderment as to the manifestations of women. They have a poor faculty for measuring feminine symptoms. Thus it repeatedly happens that for some error of demeanor a man is forced to explain, in the matter of a certain woman, that he thought she was quite another sort. A slight change in the outward marks of standard can throw a man into utter confusion. A woman may be the more resentful that another woman should choose to look like evil, but she is not so likely as the man to think the offender *is* evil.

Deducing from dress has vast precedent. Translation of the language of clothes began long before St. Paul, and has always had a deep influence upon sermons. The word "costume" itself first meant not merely clothes, but surroundings and manners, the social as well as the physical setting; so that social changes have always meant clothes changes. Tribes or races with fixed social ideas have had no fashion in the sense of a fluctuating expression. Their clothes language has been immutable. Meanings could never be mistaken. Restless, enterprising civilizations, on the other hand, have retained some liberty of action in their decorative say-so. Man got through following the lesser creatures and relinquished the glory of being the highly decorated animal. Among many of the lesser creatures the male is loud-colored and combative. Man decided to be drab and combative, and to leave the decorative to the woman. He had, literally, gone about with bells on. He tinkled, and shed diamonds.

Painting the Lily

Then he reformed. He came to hate the changes. Mr. Pepys records that King Charles made an impatient resolution to adopt a final and definitive mode in his clothes, and never to change their style again. When the periwig came in, he weakened. But he had asserted his rebellion. In the end, women were able to say of men in general, what Madame de Staël said of one man in particular, that they abused the masculine privilege of ugliness. Soldiers cut off their pigtails in 1808. A hundred years later they began the abandonment of their gold braid. Science was left to do what it could with its theory that ornament is nature's stimulus to sexual selection, and women were left to carry on the decorative traditions.

They have carried on bravely and ingeniously, with the help of men. Male poets may continue to say that loveliness needs not the foreign aid of ornament, but male dressmakers know better. If poets knew women as well as male dressmakers know them we should have profounder poetry. It is to be remarked that male dressmakers know, what so few artists in verse seem to suspect, that the essence of fashion is not form but change. The thing that is the death of verse is the life of dressmaking. A few women know the difference between style and fashion, and act as artists act when they have the same knowledge. (The difference between humor and the comic is a little harder to get at.) Yet insulting fashion is as foolish as insulting the equator. Fashion comes high, but we must go on having it. It may often be simply the cloak of cowardice, the clutch of an inferiority, but above all it is a vent for the whimsical impulses.

As whimsicality it has sometimes gone pretty far. It is judged as having gone rather far since the war. It seemed to seek the irreducible minimum in skirts,— the irate biologist snapped something about reversion to the savage loin-cloth,—yet it is apparent that the hygienists who cried out, "Thank God! no more slime-gathering skirts!" may have spoken too soon. Apparently, also, the total of clothes above the waist-line has come as close to the vanishing-point as is feasible. It never can be greatly in the interest of dressmaking, either as a business or as an art, to have the reduction go much farther. One is reminded of the description of the garments of King Shrovetide by that rascal Rabelais: "Nothing before, nothing behind, and sleeves of the same."

If there were not considerations of climate, we could not be sure how far whimsicality might venture. Because decorative fashion is by no means confined to raiment, there would be a kind of logic in regarding clothing as incidental. The women of Tonga are permitted to leave off clothes if they are tattooed. A Carib woman may go without her clothes, but not without her paint. Of late our fashionable women have frequently seemed to be on the verge of giving recognition to an identical principle. Fashion must have a corporeal basis. Hence the fashions in walking, in posture, and in figure. In Frans Hals's time fashion called for curves. To-day fashion's ideal figure has no more curves than the "Nude Descending a Staircase." I heard one woman say that when she was young, plump legs were fashionable, and hers were thin. Now that spindles were fashionable hers had become plump. But meanwhile we have obliterated age classifications. Grandma does not wear a cap. She tangoes. Hence certain prejudices. Curves suggest maturity, and maturity is as unpopular as ever it was. Maturity has money to spend, and it must be placated. All *mannequins* are lean, and fashion designs are still leaner. The dream of a woman who undulates is of an emaciated thinness, and the fashion plate hastens to show not merely the chest of a boy, but the chest of a consumptive boy. "The Song of Songs" was written a long time ago. "We have a little sister, and she hath no breasts: what shall we do for our sister in the day when she shall be spoken for?" To be flat, to circumvent the circular—this is the ideal now held up before little sister. For themselves, men have been puttering with clothes that would obliterate social differences; women have been inventing means of obliterating curve differences. To favor the heavy, the slight are receiving the supreme flattery—I refuse to erase the accidental pun. In certain other countries the fat are fashionable. On this well-fed continent reducing is discussed more frequently and with more emotion than any of the commandments or any of the statutes. The lily to be painted should, if possible, be a thin lily.

With the right figure, a woman may have concentrated attention for fashion's whisper of the Garrick epitaph: "To this complexion thou must come at last." Complexion has been standardized. It no longer needs to be earned. And in buying it there is no really embarrassing range of choice. Its elements are as portable as the elements of any other first-aid kit. Adjusting a complexion has a dressing-room origin, but it can be completed or edited anywhere. While the man pays the waiter (and the restaurant), the woman revises, accentuates and cajoles, then scrupulously reviews with the aid of her vanity-case mirror, every phase of the effect; and having corrected the ravages inflicted by the meal and the napkin, completes the ritual with a lip-stick.

Painting the Lily

Probably the lip-stick has aroused sharper critical rage than any other whimsicality of women. It can appear to have seized the feminine imagination more violently than any other specific device of fashion, and its effects, apprehended collectively, stagger an unsympathetic spectator. A whole company of scarlet lips, accompanied by a ghostly collection of white noses and shreds of negligible clothes, can, indeed, be fearfully depressing to one who doesn't quite catch the joke. In the presence of so many masks a man may find that a chance woman with clean skin has an absolutely voluptuous charm. The preparation and the carrying of these masks suggest immense labor and discomfort. But discomfort is a relativity. A man doesn't feel dressed until he is throttled by a collar. A woman doesn't feel fashionable unless something hurts. It is at the excess point that fashion consciousness begins.

In the basic grammar of the modern toilet face powder began as a means of subduing the luster of the skin. The shining face celebrated by poetry is too raw, too elemental, for a conscious art. Especially is a shiny nose resented. "If I can see my nose," said one charming woman, "I can't see anything else." Hence the powder. The esthetic consideration is accented by association. Powdering the nose having become the final preparatory action at the brink of any imaginable experience, is to be regarded as indulgently as any other of our intrinsically meaningless but useful automatisms. I recall the consternation of a brilliant woman who had reason to believe that she might be called upon to speak at a critical gathering. The final gesture was imperative, and she had mislaid her handbag. A woman seated beside her came to the rescue. "There!" cried the rescued one after a flip with the chamois, "now I can face the world!" Of course there was nothing at all the matter with her patrician nose. The physiological fact was irrelevant. Probably such irrelevancies did not exist at the beginning of the powdering practise. If a little powder suggested difference from the common face of labor, for example, a great deal of powder became an emphasis of the difference. If a little pink on the lips could restore an effect of ripe youth, a splash of vermillion could violently rebuke the hint of a youth vanished beyond recall. Presently, as in all the arts, the primitive meanings are lost sight of in effects for their own sake. The ghastliness of accentuated lips is nowhere more apparent than in the movies. Lips too red are, after all, an understandable whimsicality. But lips in the movies are black. One can see the dark gash coming, and presently is permitted to assemble the rest of the heroine.

Painting the Lily

It would be a mistake to assume that all men are revolted by these appearances. Men are notoriously fashion-bound. A man's cowardice when his woman threatens to be different from other women is too well understood to call for comment. "You've forgotten your nose," says the exacting husband, chained hopelessly to the habits of his set. And quite aside from the fashion thrall is the male enthusiasm for sex emphasis. I can recall a discussion about painted lips. One man was cynically indifferent. Two described their actual nausea when forced into the company of a bedaubed mouth. "Now, do you know," said the fourth,—I need not add that he was the youngest,—"I rather like the taste of it." People who preach to young girls about the imbecility of high heels or gauzy stockings or loud make-up, stressing the theory that good men will be repelled, and that any man attracted by the flippancies would not be worth having, are certain to stub their reformatory toes against the distressing fact that quite sane and substantial men persist in being drawn by appearances that should repulse them. I do not speak of men like Jack Lait's character, who wanted his liquor strong and his women weak, but of average male creatures with whom biology and women have, largely, to be contented.

We are to remember also that the passion for the

unreal is elementary. The face that is not really hers can be more fascinating to a girl than the loveliest natural gifts she may carry. And if this can be true of one who has gifts, how shall we chide those who have lost them or never had them? A painted face can have an exotic charm. It is essentially dirty, and it is a lot of trouble, but it escapes the realism from which most human beings find some way of turning aside.

The practical embarrassments of craving the exotic are many. Having a decorated skin as well as decorative clothes imposes enormous labor and an unremitting vigilance. Wherever fashionable and would-be fashionable feminity is assembled, the sheer work of safeguarding the effects becomes apparent. Among girls in a business office a high percentage of the gestures must be assigned to conscious and automatic amendments or verifications. Bobbed hair, theoretically an emancipation from the slavery of coils, has added new and exacting cares. In fact, bobbing can be simply a fantastic variation, intricately devised, without thought of a laborious future. Generally it seems to imply unflagging attention. The typist, after fifty words, tosses or fingers her head. After another fifty words she investigates the back of her neck. At the end of a paragraph she is free to get out the mir-

ror. Very likely most of these motions are the result
of mere nervousness. Where a man restlessly lights
a cigarette, persuading himself that he needs a moment's sedative in order to catch an idea by the tail,
the typist, bored or tired or anxious, powders her nose.
The habit has a carry-over. The presence of others
merely accentuates the impulse. Being stared at sends
a girl's hand instinctively to face or hair, or to the adjustment of garments once obscure, but now distress-
ingly familiar.

The habit of preening in public like the birds is
fixed and unabashed. In all the other arts to betray
effort is to belittle the impression. Art is told to conceal itself. The artist in face paint, certain spectacular
bobbed girls haloed like Barnum's Circassian beauty,
and a still larger group covered to some extent with
imperfectly synchronized garments, all overlook the
rule, and inspire compassion in one who does not know
enough to feel the need of perpetual revision. Many a
man (I speak with feeling) is accustomed to being
found guilty of carrying somewhere on his person
threads or hairs which other persons pick off. Do-
stoyevsky speaks of one character who always seemed
to have a bit of straw clinging to him. A man who
fancied the need to be utterly spotless, who could dream
of depriving the most eagerly solicitous philanthropists

of the opportunity to edit his appearance, would be able to visualize a kind of parallel to the situation of the preening ones.   Naturally, it would be a poor parallel. But the thought would enlarge his sympathies.   It would help him to remember about the pains of being pictorial.   The satisfactions of being pictorial he never could reach at all.

The foolish things I have said may serve to suggest that the painting of the lily, as a spectacle, receives altogether too much attention.   Spectators have some rights, including that of blundering into agonies of apprehension.   But they can make needless noises.   They should not be permitted to dwell so much on the fall of Rome.   They should be reminded, brutally if necessary, that there are other flowers in the garden.   The typical remark that "all women smoke nowadays" belongs in the category with the July or August idiocy that "everybody is out of town."   It is altogether likely that fewer than one woman in a thousand in the United States use tobacco.   There is an equally good probability that not more than one in a thousand use a lip-stick.   Impressions gathered in White Ways may be vivid and picturesque, but they are imperfectly serviceable in fixing a date for the collapse of civilization.

When lilies are painted, they are meant to be looked

at. A certain shock is part of the expectation. The instinct to give the world a mild jolt is not in itself a depravity. It is the vastly greater number of the shocked that introduces the element of weight. How the shocked may perform becomes an important part of the comedy. As usual, women continue to appear in the center of the stage, as well as on the margins. It is strictly true that they get too much attention. Somewhere, with Professor Sumner's Forgotten Man, belongs the Forgotten Woman, who does not get on the first page of the newspaper or the cover of the magazine, who does not advertise and is not discussed, who makes neither pictures nor trouble, and is content to leave lip-sticks to the harem-minded who like the job. But when she is at her best she knows that a certain amount of human advertising is a biological necessity, that nature seems to have expected the disproportion, and that if the day ever comes when women lose the spot-light of an exaggerated attention, we shall have real reason to be nervous about the fate of the race.

The Great Art Delusion

THE GREAT ART DELUSION

When the new old quarrel about bad good plays (or was it good bad plays?) so recently flamed again and the factions scurried and huddled, here screaming for more morals and there sobbing for more obscenity, one word arose above the uproar with an immemorial persistence. Sometimes it rallied, sometimes it infuriated. It could be the gonfalon and it could be the goat. In whatever image, it remained, as ever, the symbol of an eternal confusion. It was the word ART.

To repeat the word here is to challenge friendships. The poor noun bleeds. When there are no more armies or klans or congresses, when the crusading spirit has faltered to its final spark, when rebellion has become senile, Art, if properly brandished, will stir every surviving instinct for violence. Yet one good fighting word deserves another.

But a few years earlier, in the midst of a scarcely lesser turmoil, the mayor of New York was quoted as referring to "art-artists," and there was a burst of joyous derision, leveled not merely at the mayor but at all who lived in that outer darkness from which the mayor's critics assumed that he had spoken. It was permissible to speak of "dirt farmers" or of different sorts of engineer, but art-artists, it seemed to be felt, expressed a funny discrimination. That the mayor had hit upon a piece of perhaps useful terminology did not appear to be suspected. Least of all was it apparent that artists, art critics, or art connoisseurs, might have been responsible for a situation making some such discrimination a matter of practical necessity to the man in the street, if not to men in city halls, or even in art museums.

My first sharp experience of a rebellious discrimination came to me many years ago during my initiation as "art manager" of the New York *Sunday World*. An institution with an art department was to be suspected of activities harmonizing with that label, and I had entered upon my office with ambitious enthusiasm. The jolt came when my plain-spoken editor, without bitterness but without evasion, remarked, "You and I will get along fine if you don't give me any of this damned Art."

In time it became clear to me that my plain-spoken editor was quite right. He did not want the thing that was spelled with a capital. It did not matter that technically he was wrong, that the right way to express a thing is by that token the artistic way. He was thinking of filigrees, of ornament where it didn't belong, and he was wise enough to wish that when a thing needed simply to be said it would not be sung. His prejudice is widely repeated. So is obscurity as to the term Art. If that obscurity might be removed by experience; if we might go to a dictionary, to an art manager who was young enough to be sure of everything, or even to an artist who was old enough to have reached his third manner, and thereby get the last word, the case would be different. But what Art is, and who is to be called an artist, are matters more debatable than ever.

It has been easy to find a first and most obvious explanation of the confusion in modern diversity of function and in resulting subtleties of classification. We used to say "rheumatism" without encountering rebuke. One requires a medical education and some brashness to use the term to-day. Speaking by the card becomes an increasingly nice matter. To the plain man the result is bewildering. The plain man looks at a painting and asks, "Is this art?" No, he is told, this is not art. It tells a story. It is literary. The plain man looks at a book and asks, "Is this art?" And again the answer is No. This, he learns, is only propaganda. Should the plain man go back and discover that *Don Quixote* and *The Tale of a Tub* and *Pilgrim's*

The Great Art Delusion

Progress were all of them propaganda and therefore not art, he would be in a fair way to reach an utterly modern confusion of mind. Where the plain man halts, convinced that he never can know what it is all about, the cognoscenti begin, and the simple truth is that they have reached a bewilderment as great as his.

The whole art question has been fearfully muddled. Honest artists and honest critics have, sometimes with genuine ingenuity, sometimes with nothing better than a strong-arm belligerency, struggled to clear up the mess. Yet we seem to get deeper into the mire of the thing. And none of us escapes. The question is not an academic subtlety. Art touches all of us, and art questions, grotesquely remote as they may be made to appear, are matters of common concern. When books are reviewed, when paintings are appraised, when public works are under discussion, when plays are subjected to the pull and haul of professional and popular debate, we may begin to see that confused thinking about art, its privileges and its obligations, when this confused thinking begins to objectify itself, is not a remote matter, calamitous only to hair-splitting highbrow specialists, but a matter vital to human comfort. The poor magistrates, for example, who would, I have no doubt, like to be considered as practical men, are quite evidently in a state of bitter perplexity about art.

The Great Art Delusion

They have reason to wish that art could be kept out of court. Evidently it can not be kept out of court unless it can be kept out of life. Since not only our statutory intrusions and our public instruction but our amusements are constantly affected by notions of art, since we seemed doomed to be kept dodging missiles in the brawl between art theorists on the one hand and give-them-what-they-want theorists on the other, both sides full of disgust for "them," it can not be grossly reprehensible to ask if there is not some way in which the problem, always with us, may be simplified a little.

It would be interesting to discover that word-looters were the real culprits in the quarrel, to find, once more, that stealing the appointed clothing of an idea is no small sin against human peace. Many a revolution has started by a Raffles.

You may have decided that following this word "art" through the rank jungle of speculation isn't worth the trouble. In the interest of those who may have abandoned the pursuit let me leap intermediate escapades by quoting the most delightful extremist. There are plenty of extremists, but Mr. Clive Bell has such a gentlemanly way of insulting the accepted, he can be so graciously contemptuous, and he can state the obscure with such charming clearness, that he may well be the spokesman of the art-artists.

The Great Art Delusion

Mr. Bell tells us that "the cold white peak of art" is reached in "significant form." This need not be startling even to the profane outsider until he learns what Mr. Bell means by significant form. We are told that, to be significant, form must mean nothing that can possibly bear a name or that in any way can be associated with anything else. "To appreciate a work of art we need bring with us nothing from life, no ideas and affairs, no familiarity with its emotions. Art transports us from the world of man's activity to a world of esthetic exaltation. . . . We are lifted above the stream of life." Nothing thinkable is to be represented. "Every sacrifice made to representation is something stolen from art." To understand this sort of art "we need to know nothing whatever about history." In fact, "we require nothing but sensibility." Recognition of a correspondence between the forms of a work of art and the familiar forms of life "can not possibly provoke esthetic emotion. Only significant form can do that."

You will guess that all so-called works of art that *tell* anything except the sheer ecstasy of the artist are here brushed aside for good and all. If you *recognize* a single trace, the jig is up. Beholding a painting by Ingres, for example, Mr. Bell perceives human beings. Thumbs down for Ingres. "We do not see the figures as forms, because we immediately think of them as people." Horrors!—*people!* The forms must be devised so that they will have no possible associational import. "All informatory matter is irrelevant and should be eliminated." Thus a picture like *The Doctor*—in the pitiful story-telling category—"not being a work of art has none of the immense ethical value possessed by all objects that provoke esthetic ecstasy."

Turning from the pictorial, Mr. Bell remarks that at a concert, "incapable of feeling the austere emotions of art, I begin to read into the musical forms human emotions of terror and mystery, love and hate, and to spend the minutes, pleasantly enough, in a world of turbid and inferior feeling."

In view of this experience we need not be astonished to find Mr. Bell asking, "Why should artists bother about the fate of humanity" when "rapture suffices?" In other words, it is only by not having meaning that forms or sounds can have significance. Yet when he turns to literature (it is only a turn) he remarks, oddly, that "writers with nothing to say soon come to regard the manipulation of words as an end in itself," which surely might seem like an unclubable fling at Gertrude Stein.

But the "white peak" of the art Mr. Bell is thinking of is not wholly isolated. Another peak, perhaps not wholly white, is permitted to religion. He admits that art has existed as a religion concurrent with other religions. However, to reach this high proximity religion must have "nothing to do with intellectual beliefs." Other religions are admitted into ecstatic relationship only upon condition that they regard their ecstasy as an end in itself. There is the assumption that what we call religion, if countenanced at all, has no better status than that of a poor relation; for, with an earnestness that must leave us in no doubt of the writer's ardor of conviction, he says that "art is the most universal and the most permanent form of religious expression."

Of course Mr. Bell is talking about sublimated esthetics. I relinquish the task of discussing whether significance without association is a sane proposal; whether we can carry to anything whatever an emotion not derived from life; whether there can be a single theory of beauty on which nature does not hold the patent; whether any unparented ecstasy can lift itself by its bootstraps and be more or less than natural. Nor is there space to consider all of the things Mr. Bell doesn't like because he does like the art-artists; his notion that museums of art are a horror; that "cultivated parents cultivate their children; thousands of wretched little creatures are daily being taught to love the beautiful"—and so on. I am concerned at the moment not with Mr. Bell's innocent plea for the sufficiency of an irresponsible esthetic joy, but with the brisk way in which he scampers up his cool peak with that word "art."

It is true that the meaning of a word is to be ascertained not by its ancestry or previous condition of servitude but by the reaction it produces. It is true also that words are elected; which implies that they mean what we permit them to mean. Before letting the word "art" vanish into the mists, it is fair to ask whether fundamental every-day needs may not make it worth while to acknowledge the basic blunder in the common as well as in the transcendental use of this word.

The great art delusion, responsible for confusing reactions and endless fumblings in analysis, is that art the *expression* and art the *thing* can be named by the use of a single term. Whatever we may agree to call the expression of ideas and emotions, it ought to be plain that this is but one of the elements of a so-called work of art. If we use the word art to name the *way* a thing is done, we can not, without perpetuating our confusions, go on flatly labeling the *thing* as art.

The artist + his idea + his expression = a work

of art. In such a formula—I make no apology for its elementariness—the word "art" belongs to the element of expression. To apply the word to the element of expression is to give clarity to the use of the word, and to promise a better clarity for our thinking about the work of art. Personality is not art. Ideas are not art. Imagination is not art. Highly original minds exist without a sense of art. Of all the highly original ideas with which we become acquainted by some form of communication few are expressed with any art knowledge or intention. The *conscious communication* of personality, of emotions and ideas, is art, and the *medium* by which the communication is accomplished is *an* art. Mr. Santayana's phrase has it that the idea is the essence. All transcendentalism is a search for essences. Perhaps the same might be said of all true philosophy. Mr. Bell finds the uttermost essence in a created shape.

Looking at a work of art with such a formula in mind would have some profitable results. We should be able to estimate the art on its own account as worthy or unworthy of the artist and his subject. We should be able to admit freely that art is essentially and necessarily unmoral, which would be an immense comfort to certain people. Only an art that is irresponsible, as pliantly irresponsible as a pen or brush, can serve the purposes of mediumship. It is not the art but the artist that is responsible. No formula can save the artist from responsibility. The more completely irresponsible we make the art the greater becomes the responsibility of the artist it serves. The more important we make the figure of the artist in the world, the more profoundly certain is it that he will be held to account. He will be held to account not only for his art but for his ideas. In this respect he will be in the same boat with other men. None of us can hope or decently wish to escape participation in the obligations of human association. If priests of the religions which Mr. Bell has exalted to an equality, or a near-equality, with his religion of significant form are not released either by their own code or by social expectation, from the ethical imperatives resting upon their fellow creatures, I can not see why a priesthood of esthetics, even one strangely disposed not to bother about humanity, should be coddled in a temple consecrated to delirium. I have never known a man-size artist who asked any such boon.

A French painter once produced a picture showin a heap of bloody entrails on a marble slab. The art was admittedly exquisite, but a critic who refused to be fuddled by a bifurcated word would have had no difficulty in perceiving that the quality of the art made the work of art the nastier. A man capable of exquisite art could have expressed anything. And he chose entrails. Emerson's saying that no object is so foul that intense light will not make it beautiful, was a tribute to the power of art. But foulness still needs an explanation if not an excuse. Thus, while a thing is not indecent because a moron thinks it is, neither is a blackguardism to be sanctified by a sonnet.

To glorify the illuminating power of art is to fasten upon the artist, in any field, an accountability that can not be dislodged. Art is an *act*, and no one has ever advanced a satisfactory reason why artists should not, like other persons, be subject to consideration for their acts. If anything foul is chosen for either the accusing or the mitigating illumination of art, the artist must accept estimate of his choice, and he will never get much sympathy by urging that he only wanted to show his art. I see beauty as the *form* of truth; art as carrying the theology of beauty; technique as the ritual of art. As no gorgeousness of ritual could glorify a make-believe religion, no beauty of garment can lift from the artist the onus of his gesture. He himself will always hover in his picture or in his book. Because all creation is confession, no objectivity of method can obliterate the artist. No splendor of the idea-package can soften our chagrin if we find nothing inside, or if the contents accuse the artist and insult us.

Art that does not say something may have the ruminative satisfactions inherent in whittling a stick or the practise importance of musical scales, but it is no part of a work of art. I resort to the obvious by way of emphasizing the less trite (though no longer new) contention that art is essentially *communication*. Expression may need no audience to give pure joy to one who expresses. Expression is elementally natural. Functionally the artist is separated and distinguished by the fact that consciously and by devoted preparation he expresses to *communicate* his joy. Only communication, only the exultation of sharing, can give a work of art its occasion; and if communication is basic, the value of the thing said comes under consideration with the value of the way of saying it. Thus, the offense of a theory that ignores all but the art element, is to be measured by the circumstance that all works of art imply audience or spectators. A work of art may be created without social thought, yet the mind of the artist and all other elements entering into his work are social products; from which we must deduce that every art medium is a product not only of use but of response. To say that a responding recognition is implicit in the language of every art, is answer enough to any pose of indifference. It is quite easy to understand a savage contempt for the conduct of audiences, to be appalled by profundities of ignorance, to feel humiliation in watching flippancies of choice, to be amazed by complacent insensibility to beauty, but the sculptor must go on with the estimate of the angle from which his statue is to be *seen,* the musician and the actor must be interested in the acoustics, the writer must continue to be concerned not only in mentally objectifying his emotions but in communicating them intelligibly. To find that not only technique but emotions and ideas must be affected by the implied respondent is to learn, as men in other fields of human activity inevitably learn, that restraints and inspiration come from the same source—that an art with no object outside itself is no more thinkable than a love or a pity with no object outside itself.

It is not at all likely that any artist's decision not to bother about humanity has ever been responsible in any discernible degree for humanity's habit of not bothering about art. But doctrines of special privilege, esthetic fanaticisms and a general effect of inacessibility must have had some influence. These must on occasion have resulted in decisions to let art go on with its own dervish dance. It is the instinct of the mass to permit a withdrawing priesthood to flock as it will. A better doctrine of art's responsibility to life might, despite despairing theories of a common stupidity and inertia, have a real influence upon humanity. When we say of a work of art, in printed pages or on canvas, that it "endures" we can mean nothing more than that it continues to be recognized. However it may be born, art "lives" by response. Great art, like other great deeds, may be obliterated. The highest greatness in any deed disregards this hazard, yet the potential in recognition can never be ignored. The appreciation of art and all that it carries is so vital to a civilization that is ever to deserve the name that we can not afford to dismiss any truculence or peevishness or pride that may work against it.

These contentions might seem merely academic if we overlooked their possible service in reducing a common confusion. If before a poem or a picture or any other work of art, we accept our privilege to consider the distinct elements of personality, of ideas, of expression as likely to be of varying significance, we may escape a bewilderment that specialists as well as laymen often seem to feel when they try to think of the total or talk of the total as a singleness. We may, for example, thereby be able more frequently to see that a thing beautifully *done* is not always a beautiful *thing*— as in the cracking of a safe. Keeping the integrity of our sense of art will leave us freer to judge that idea-essence with which art makes its bargain. The interplay of impulses originating in character, temperament, situation, art instinct, is too complicated to be summed up in any diagram. And imagination rides like a king among all the other factors. We do not know what happens when the artist "listens in," whether the illumination may rightly be said to come from within or without. We stand before an eternal mystery. But a right formula is helpful for the same reason that a wrong one is hurtful. A formula that tries to make a work of art fit into an "art" measure is doomed to failure.

Of course we should not need a formula. Beauty is more important than any logic about it; but recognizing the duality of art and idea, does no injustice to either; it may do better justice to both. Recognizing the beauty of an idea may make us tolerant of a deficiency in the expression. If the idea fails for us, we may have reason to regard the art as a mitigation. We may find personality transcending either. An artist with real greatness of personality may remain to the end of his days a poor artist. We may regret that individual greatness lacks communicative power, that its artist side is inferior, but we should not be tricked by any interest in art or in works of art, into measuring personality by art-power alone. On the other hand, an individual with art-power may not choose or be able to offer for embodiment an idea-essence at all commensurate with either the bigness of his personality or the beauty in his expression. He may be original or merely be different. He may *see* originally and express tritely. The thing he sees may be insignificant, and he may have a genius for showing us how beautiful an insignificant thing may be made when he expresses it—how beautiful anything is that he *does*. Whatever the situation, we shall be better off, either in forming a judgment or in transmitting a judgment, if we have escaped the delusion that the single element, art, can possibly characterize all that a work of art leaves us to feel or to consider. Art may dominate the impression—that is, the glory of its privilege—but we can not wholly estimate the king by his clothes.

The need for a term that will less clumsily cover "work of art" is stressed by the need to leave art itself free—by the fact that art will stay free whether we will or no. Shakespeare was always an artist; Leonardo we can not rightly estimate in the same terms. The Gettysburg Address had beautiful art. We must remain free to appreciate the art of one who is always an artist, of one who is more than an artist, of one not an artist who has the gift for using an art. We can complete no equation without such clearness. We can not ignore the man, the idea, the occasion, in explaining an emotion. On the other hand, sheer art beauty is a reality however it may be hurt by the company it keeps. An illicit idea—like preaching where it does not belong—may invalidate a work of art without invalidating the art. If we ever come to forget the propaganda we may again think of the total as a work of art. A work of art sold, even as an afterthought, to the purposes of salesmanship, loses its work of art significance, though it can not thereby lose its art. Much of the best art craftsmanship of to-day is used in advertising. This may be heartbreaking to lovers of art, even if it is a great boon to salesmanship. It may be wickeder to paint a flattering picture of a corporation's product for the corporation's dollars than to paint a flattering portrait of the duke's mistress for the duke's florins. It may be that men used to paint more madonnas not because they were more religious but because there was a better market for madonnas. Evidently men who practise art without recompense should cast the first stone.

Some day we shall find the true dividing line that separates the "commercial," that marks the work of art difference and the ethical difference between painting an exhibition portrait of the millionaire's stupid wife for money and painting a sales convention portrait of the millionaire's patented mowing machine for money; between the situation of the writer who thinks of a large audience in terms of work-of-art influence and one who thinks of a large audience in terms of profit only. However the sordidness of the world may weigh upon those who cherish dreams of a perfected expression, an unhampered truth, an undefiled beauty, there is a consolation affecting, if not our immediate distresses, at least our sense of destination, that Time eliminates every quibble as to the circumstances of production. The real work of art (it will ultimately get a name)—the work blending in its total the spirit of the artist, the vitality of the idea, and the essential art—may rear itself at last from the ruck, may come to the judgment of answering emotions, without its chains. It is a pity that we should heap so many obscurations about to-day's madonnas while agreeing, for example, to forget why Doctor Johnson hurried with Rasselas.

Probably we shall never have clearness of thinking in these matters until there is a wider and deeper recognition of the truth that all arts, fine and otherwise, are subsidiary to the supreme art of living. At the white peak of the art of living is the essence of essences. Any theory that sets up a super-art, especially one that affects to despise life, is essentially evasive and dishonest. Logically it should begin with suicide. It is "striking on the job"—an intellectual sabotage. In a creed acknowledging the art of living there is no place for brotherhoods of irresponsible ecstasy, but there is room—there is demand—for the uttermost triumphs of expression, for every individual thought or emotion which the common heritage of art language may carry to mankind, and for the artist as a full participator in the common struggle, though he be necessarily aloof, like other of his life-brothers, for the creative hours. The indifference of the world has no greater burden for the artist than for the laborer, the inventor or the preacher. The artist, as life's spokesman, has, indeed, certain gentlemanly obligations, among these that of not talking too much about himself. Too much art is about art. Too much history is about history rather than about life.

Whatever may be figured as the impulsions of art in the past, art consciousness in the future will draw closer to life. Havelock Ellis has been speaking of dancing as "the loftiest, the most moving, the most beautiful of the arts, because it is no mere translation or abstraction from life; it is life itself." No right to esthetic joy is withheld or diminished in significance by the insistence, as by Mr. Ellis, that the esthetic sense

The Great Art Delusion

is a social necessity. It is a social necessity for reasons resting in its social origin. That beauty needs life is part of the imperative that life needs beauty. Life and the artist need each other—desperately. Life is still appallingly ugly. Art still has selfish futilities. Like formulated religion, like coordinated government, it will learn that keeping close to life is a condition of survival. Life's blunders in trying to get along without its committees because government has been bad, without religion because churches have been ineffectual, without art because certain artists have wanted a separate god, lifts no responsibility from the shoulders of men and women capable of a devoted leadership.

I have said art "consciousness." Let my postscript make it plain that I have no faith looking to an enduring value for works of art in any conscious appeal to the general. I am no such optimist, as to either art or the general. But a great art may begin with an artist-consciousness of humanity, with a sharing sense of life's ironies, without truckling on the way. Though art be *addressed*, no theory of dread duty can force the artist to address the great group. He may reach it. Whispers of individual expression have, by a miracle in which there is more of what we call chance than most of us find it ethical to admit, reverberated to the ends of the earth. An artist may attain his best art in thinking of an infinite audience. He may attain it in thinking simply of another self. It may be wrung from him in moments of lonesome exasperation. Certainly we can not hope that it will germinate in a philosophy of irresponsibility or of contempt. History seems to show that while little men sometimes have big expression-gifts, really great works of art are made by great men, and great men—well, they are great *men*.

Quarrel Texts

QUARREL TEXTS

THE DOUBLE STANDARD

THAT men did devise the moralities, and that they made a thoroughly male job of it, was a feminist discovery which at one time received hysterical attention. "Man-made" figured in the slogan of a great rebellion. It began to appear that enormous readjustments must happen. After proper changes as to voting and office-holding and jury service had been attended to, something was to be done as to the really elemental matter of sex discrimination. Men and women were to be placed on the same footing, however slippery the footing might be. The reminder that it was Nature who invented the double standard did not halt the rush of events. It was too late to sue Nature. While a strictly technical guilt could not be proved, men were found to be horribly guilty just the same. If they had not invented the arrangement they had stolen the patent.

Naturally most men did not feel driven into a corner. Most men knew only that a daughter's sin might be much more inconvenient than a son's sin, and, knowing this, they spent such time as they might give to the subject not in blaming Nature for being invidious, but in tinkering with measures for avoiding the personal inconvenience. A husband, as a kind of viceroy of Behavior, became, like the father, a simple pragmatist. He noted that Nature seemed to take no offense at a Solomon with a hundred wives. On the other hand, he observed Nature's angry way of indicating that a woman must not love plurally. He might not go so far as to regard this as outrageously discriminatory. Generally he was content to act upon the basis of an existing order. As usual, he said to himself, social prejudice has a biological antecedent. Civilization is codified convenience.

Meanwhile, since we were, theoretically, tethered to a natural Constitution that could not be amended (science's experiments in sex reversal had not yet begun), certain alleviatory measures were adopted. Some of these might have looked like a punishment for the offense of being male. To do men justice, a great many of these penalties were devised by men themselves. The sarcasm of alimony supplemented the husbandly obligation of perpetual support. If it was the business of sociology to correct the mistakes of biology, there was logic in the jury-box slogan: When in doubt, bleed him good. So many men deserved to be bled that the effect of a tax upon maleness may have been at least debatably just.

But none of these expedients stifled the hated double standard tradition which the late social revolution met head on. There was open repudiation of the insult in all legal sops. Sin was to have no sex. Morality stared and wondered whether this meant that men were to be better or women worse. There were indeed moralists who made a sincere plea for a new practise which should demolish the sophistries behind which men have been hiding since history began. But there were also rebels claiming to represent an aggrieved sex who insisted that taming men would only beg the question. The last remaining citadel of inequality was to be taken not by giving men less liberty but by giving women more.

Thus ended the era from which it is assumed that we have fully emerged. There are no evidences of the promised feminine dictatorship; only of the usual American feminine initiative, the established submissiveness of the American man, scolded by the reactionaries as if he were a Tom Jones, and jeered by the radicals as if he were a Joseph Andrews. The crusaders' shrill cries for liberty have subsided. What has happened? What is the meaning of the awful silence? Is there a new morality, or a new immortality? Has society become honest at the expense of its honor, or only logical at the expense of its sense of humor? Will women, in General Sherman's mood, find that only one thing is so terrible as a defeat and that is a victory? Or was it all a manner of speaking, a *post bellum* joke, slightly acidulous but without profundity, no more momentously indicative than cosmetics?

It would, perhaps, be better to regard the questions as flippant than to press them. If only the noisy incited the interrogation only the noisy would answer. Probably women never will succeed in implicating Woman. There will continue to be two sexes, more or less. Ethical crises are no more changed by the circumstance that some men are not at all male than by the collateral circumstance that some women are not at all female. In any case, there will always be pushers who favor the greatest annoyance to the greatest number. Only Nature, who has no fashion but only style, will be found sitting pretty at the last.

FACTS

He was a lawyer—and one of those charming lawyers—who told me he had no time for current print (he indicated, in particular, newspapers and periodicals), because he was devoutly committed, by taste and by conscience, to facts. And where, I asked him, did he find these facts? In history, he said.

"You mean," I suggested, "that facts are between stiff covers."

Not that, he assured me. Not merely the form guided him. He wanted the considered, the sifted things, the things that stood up after the hubbub was over. The plain hard facts.

He was a lawyer, concerned with testimony and authentic evidence, yet it became plain that he was willing to say facts. He believed sincerely that there were such things, and they were to be found in certain places, and not in certain other places. He knew that what the judge handed down was called an opinion, that what a law means is determined not by the statute but by these subsequent opinions, that these opinions would be used in forming further opinions. He knew that the term decision implies opinion. He knew that facts are left to the jury, and that the jury hands over a collective opinion. Yet he could say "facts" quite without any effect of regarding the medium as simply one more phase of opinion.

I learned that he did not regard a historian as a witness speaking chiefly, often wholly, from hearsay. I saw that to-day's newspaper is a delusion, but that a history written from a file of the *London Times* is a different matter. Renan has given it as the law of Oriental history writing that one book should annihilate its precedessor, so that the sources of a compilation rarely survive the compilation itself; which is equivalent to showing that the original say-so is always debatable, while the quoted say-so begins the hardening process that goes with the molding of "facts."

The loose reasoning of those who hunt for tight facts might sometimes seem of negligible interest if new criticism of life and art did not so frequently seek to bully us with assumptions of finality. Incidentally, the dead appear to be more credible than the living, as if time embalmed an opinion into a stiffness worthy to wear a firmer name. That all possible history is only opinion should be evident enough to check arrogance of quotation, yet the bludgeon falls, quite in the old manner, upon the hapless head of living expression. Dead and living might have no disparity of rights if their common frailty were admitted, but if mere ossification in the integument of past opinion is to carry superior rights, especially when it has just been exhumed, the living must suffer a sharp disadvantage. The lusty will escape. There is, as usual, a defense in seeing the joke. And there are excellent advantages in being alive. But the waste of time and printer's ink, the confusion of issues, the spectacle of "fact"-

repressed minds, the litter of junk in the path of common thinking, contribute to our resentment. Science is decent enough about saying nebular hypothesis or binominal theorem. Two-dimension men and women, plain and fancy, want the facts. They want the facts about the war or the correct way to set a dinner table. If you tell them that words, like collars and card rules, are elected, and that everybody has a vote, they may not call you a juggler but they will hunt a heaven and hell, black and white, good and bad, right and wrong authority ignorant enough and wise enough to be positive. They want to know whether this is a good book or a good play, which is a matter very different from wishing for an opinion, and there always will be fact-dispensers to give them the comfort of an unqualified classification.

We must have school books, and perhaps they must always be concocted by fact-writers. Any one who has answered the nine hundredth question of a child discovers that the fact road is easier than the opinion road, and that there can be no glamour in a person who isn't sure. Grown-up children exert the same pressure, eternally nourishing the mountebank and the quack.

Quarrel Texts

The ennobling of ancestors is, perhaps, one of those rituals of self-satisfaction upon which we should hesitate to intrude. Our quarrelsome country has had a variety of founders and their investiture is a natural feature of dramatized gratitude. Nothing is more favoring to stability than a standardized sentiment as to the pioneers. It is only when forefathers are indicated as having had *intentions* that we begin to catch a hint of our common hazard, that we begin to see how the designs of the dead may carry for the living an eternally statutory implication. In one part of the country or another, at feast or funeral, in homage to strangely dissonant beginners, each with jealous gods, we hear it commented that this sort of country isn't what the founders meant at all. It is as if, in the matter, let us say, of Rome, the spirit of Romulus, or of the wolf, were to protest to Mussolini that he was missing the point.

Countries have, indeed, been governed by ghosts, but there is scarcely a parallel to the American confusion arising from the geographically discordant sets, each voiced by descendants who have, on occasion, found the others guilty of sacramental impudence, if not of downright bad taste. Many a group of adventurers, some of them not especially prayerful, has been burdened not only with the onus of fixing the future of a continent in general terms, but of specifically transmitting the private rules of an original going concern for the regulation of the vast subsequent trust. Celebrators of varying territorial dialects have seemed to be willing to prove if they could that delusions of grandeur are not a wholly modern development. With French and Spanish founders, with Dutch founders bringing free schools and other democratic radicalisms, with Puritan founders planting the prickly seed of abnegation, with later 'Forty-niners and other protagonists of the punch, we have been equipped for quarrels of precedence. The social rivalries of a Puritan Back Bay, a Dutch Four Hundred, a Liberty Bell aristocracy and a Washingtonian Virginia have illustrated the predicament.

New England cleverly wrote the school books. All hands joined in the persuasive selling talk. Every race and every creed were to be welcomed through an open door. When the promissory note called a Constitution fell due, it turned out that the selling talk had been Pickwickian. The door was officially slammed shut at last, and a brilliant logic defended the announcement that all the rooms were full. Meanwhile some one had devised the hideous melting pot. Naturally there was a row over who was to own the pot and a more acrimonious uproar over the discovery that it held a founders' dye. Under the circumstances it is a bit astonishing that there has not been more frequent and more violent complaint that the country is not as advertised. In frank indifference to any such consideration early publicity is repudiated, but one may gather from memorial eloquence that early "intentions" are still subject to respectable quotation. The game of a Promised Land and a nonpartisan brotherhood, proud of its diversities, had a good start. The joker was some founder's intention. That card is played in the crisis of any theoretical anxiety. It is a wonderful trick-taker. Its mutations are mesmeric. If we are not moving as somebody intended, every inferiority complex clutches at guidance. Timidity is told that the founders *knew*. The founders were foreigners. Set a founder to catch a founder. The old chap with the store teeth who spits on the stove at the post-office has an outspoken opinion of the new gang that is trying to run the village. This wasn't how it was to be. We are drifting wildly. Letting in a lot of outsiders who don't know their place, who won't see that the other foreigners knew what was best—what was *going* to be best. Moreover, these first foreigners became American at once. Modern foreigners are menacingly slow about reforming. They show no sense of the need to hurry the process of being dyed. And they breed, which means more imperfectly dyed Americans.

Yet we all love the founders. Perhaps some of us feel the way Emerson said the folks of the neighborhood felt about Thoreau. They all loved Henry, but they didn't like him. Some of us don't like the founders—at board meetings and banquets. All of them didn't have descendants, but they must have known that they might have them, and that if they did the descendants would talk.

The ideal founder would express hopes, devout or otherwise, and should be forgiven for any plucky effort to make these seem worthy of him. But he would specifically (in writing) release posterity from servitude toward the elocution of descendants, lineal or sentimental. Reading intentions in the original might not assure imitative approval, yet it would give the founder a fair field and some favor.

How Old is Genius?

HOW OLD IS GENIUS?

In the matter of art, youth and age often hold
fears that have more than a superficial likeness. We
find age, for example, betraying apprehensiveness as
to birthday prejudices and a slipping attention on the
part of its audience. Youth's anxiety is equally associated with the horrible haste of the clock. To youth,
nothing looks worth while unless it can be induced to
happen soon.

When I was nineteen, it had become quite clear to
me that if I were not famous at twenty-five the jig
would be up. Naturally I had no suspicion of my triteness. If we knew that we had happened before, our
necessary impudence would be crippled. Even a taste
of fame can not appease the newly adult suspicion of
the management. Max Beerbohm was having fun with
this state of mind when, thirty years ago, he declared,
"I shall write no more." Emerson's youthful, "Good-
bye, proud world, I'm going home," might suggest a
rich anthology of sophomoric impatiences. I was not
considering the misgivings of better men. I had an

anxiety, and it was documented. All the names were at hand, a sort of who's who among the early.

At twenty-five I had a new list, a larger list, of the great whose blaring entrance into the arena had occurred somewhere within a ten-year period ending at thirty-five. This, I said, to my Unconscious, is your last stand. Win now or crawl into obscurity and pull the hole after you. But at thirty-five there had been neither apocalypse nor cataclysm, and I was too busy to fulfill the pledged abasement. The crawling was postponed. Moreover, new testimony had been introduced. Evidently the imposing triumphs marking the period between thirty-five and forty-five made most of the earlier records seem if not trivial at least inconclusive. And there came a time when it became imperative to acknowledge that the "curve" of genius rose sharply on the way toward fifty-five, while not merely mature masterpieces but initial entrances of the most distinguished order were not to be included unless a still larger curve could be drawn.

It was not until the other day, in one of those intervals so plainly marked for unproductiveness that any maundering or mischief is likely to be invited, that I ventured to look among the records, no longer with an eagerness to be confirmed, nor altogether with a swagger of assurance, but with what seemed to be an amiable curiosity as to the possible insolence of the facts. No need to consider sheer precocity, which so often has an effect described (by George Eliot, for instance,) as resembling the predicament of one who gets up too early and is sleepy all the afternoon. On the other hand, it could make no point to show genius still going strong at eighty-five or ninety. There are inverted prodigies that upset all orderly calculations. I chose, arbitrarily, to look for the signs not of a first significant expression but of the fully "arrived" creative effort—not for the first affairs but for the high moods of authentic gestation. Perhaps I thereby begged the question, for genius has no code for getting itself said. An *Endymion* written at twenty-one and a *Way of All Flesh* written at sixty-six both represented guilt in obeying that impulse, and each in its way illustrated sustained power. It was the hundred-yard dash that I chose to ignore, not because this offered a lesser sign, in itself, but because the longer run, if not the marathon, seems more likely to eliminate the element of chance, which art is quite privileged to use, yet which can be no part of its true essence. Mere length is not, then, an art quality, but it can be demonstrative. It has been said of well-cleaners in Africa that they must be able to stay submerged (with halted lungs) for four or five minutes, and that men under

sixty are found not to have the necessary endurance.
There is scarcely a happy parallel in the case of creative effort, though we might find many instances of
short-winded talent to bolster an analogy.

It would be easy, yet quite unscientific, to assume
that the time theoretically required to produce a novel
makes the novel the severest test of either the scope or
the intensity of power. Sustained thinking and feeling and expressing can have no such measure. I found
myself looking up the novels (and romances) as well
as certain outstanding plays, with no logic whatever,
though I might, if I had felt any obligation, have
argued that in a novel a writer has wider latitude for
the betrayal of weaknesses than is offered in any other
medium. It was impossible to miss the revelation that
poets and playwrights are likely to flower earlier than
the novelists. Here were the *School for Scandal* at
twenty-six, *Every Man in His Humor* at twenty-five,
The Beaux' Stratagem at twenty-nine, *Vor Sonnenaut-
gang* at twenty-six, not to speak of Belasco's *May
Blossom* at twenty-five. Ibsen's *Doll's House* at fifty
or the *Philoctetes,* produced when Sophocles was well
on toward ninety, did not seem to invalidate a theory
that the playwright might be as early as the poet.

The twenties, I am bound to admit, offered poor
pickings, though Kipling and Stephen Crane (*The Red*

How Old is Genius?

Badge of Courage was written at twenty-five) and many another are to be cited in support of any claim for real youth. I have confessed a juvenile theory as to twenty-five. A later excursion into figures resulted at one moment in the conviction that thirty-six was a noble crisis, for here was Shakespeare with *Hamlet,* Flaubert with *Madame Bovary,* Irving with *Rip Van Winkle,* Boccaccio with *Decameron,* Whitman with *Leaves of Grass,* Poe with *The Raven,* Stevenson with *Dr. Jekyll.* But in the end all such fantastic hypotheses were toppled.

Let me offer, with any proper apology for casualness, some of my notations, decade by decade. There is every likelihood of inexactness, for it is not always possible to discriminate accurately between writing date and publication date. And there is plenty of room for quarrel as to the choice of genius's "high spot." The entrance of a new personality inevitably attracts more attention than any later gesture. Loose criticism often confuses the furor of surprise with the sound of a real triumph, though first furors are, I suppose, in themselves a triumph. In a matter so elementally a question of opinion I should not and do not bother to consider how closely my choice of any book may match another choice. Nevertheless, I have not, to my own feeling, chosen with any flagrant peculiarity of preference.

How Old is Genius?

In the thirties: Shakespeare, *Hamlet,* (36); Flaubert, *Madame Bovary,* (37); Whitman, *Leaves of Grass,* (36); Boccaccio, *Decameron,* (36); Sue, *Mysteries of Paris,* (39); Stevenson, *Dr. Jekyll,* (36); Wilkie Collins, *The Woman in White,* (36); Gogol, *Dead Souls,* (33); Frank Norris, *The Pit,* (32); Kipling, *Kim,* (35); Page, *Marse Chan,* (34); Eggleston, *Hoosier Schoolmaster,* (34); Garland, *Rose of Dutcher's Coolly,* (35); Cable, *Dr. Sevier,* (39); D'Annunzio, *Francesca Da Rimini,* (39); Wycherley, *The Plain Dealer,* (33); Crawford, *Saracenesca,* (33); Poole, *The Harbor,* (35); Merrimée, *Columba,* (37); Hergesheimer, *Java Head,* (38).

In the forties: Chaucer, *Canterbury Tales,* (46); Barrie, *Peter Pan,* (43); Balzac, *La Cousine Bette,* (46); Tolstoy, *Anna Karénina,* (42); Molière, *Le Misanthrope,* (44); Scott, *St. Ronan's Well,* (43); Dickens, *Great Expectations,* (49); Thackeray, *The Newcomes,* (43); Jane Austen, *Emma,* (40); Dostoievsky, *Crime and Punishment,* (44); Mark Twain, *Huckleberry Finn,* (48); Shaw, *Man and Superman,* (47); George Eliot, *Adam Bede,* (40); Howells, *Silas Lapham,* (47); Anatole France, *Thais,* (45); Rabelais, *Pantagruel,* (42); Blackmore, *Lorna Doone,* (44); Dante, *The Divine Comedy,* (41); Sudermann, *Es War,* (47); Dumas, *Monte Cristo,* (42); Daudet,

142

How Old is Genius?

Sapho, (44); Fielding, *Tom Jones*, (41); George Moore, *Esther Waters*, (41); Trollope, *Barchester Towers*, (42); George Sand, *La Mare au Diable*, (42); Zola, *La Terre*, (48); Hewlett, *The Queen's Quair*, (42); Smollett, *Humphrey Clinker*, (49); Stowe, *Uncle Tom's Cabin*, (41); Conrad, *Lord Jim*, (43); Deland, *The Awakening of Helena Ritchie*, (48); Melville, *Moby Dick*, (42); Burnett, *A Lady of Quality*, (46); Dreiser, *The Genius*, (43); Wilson, *Bunker Bean*, (44); Tarkington, *Seventeen*, (46); Galsworthy, *Fraternity*, (42); Hale, *The Man Without a Country*, (41); Willa Cather, *My Antonia*, (41); Edith Wharton, *The House of Mirth*, (42); James Lane Allen, *The Choir Invisible*, (46); Sherwood Anderson, *Poor White*, (43).

In the fifties: Sterne, *Sentimental Journey*, (55); Goethe, *Faust*, (59); Meredith, *The Egoist*, (58); Hardy, *Tess*, (50); Ibsen, *A Doll's House*, (50); Wells, *Mr. Britling*, (50); Turgueniev, *Virgin Soil*, (59); Racine, *Athalie*, (51); Milton, *Paradise Lost*, (55); Hawthorne, *The Marble Faun*, (55); Cervantes, *Don Quixote*, (57); Bunyan, *Pilgrim's Progress*, (50); Gautier, *Le Capitaine Fracasse*, (52); Swift, *Gulliver's Travels*, (58); Stockton, *Mrs. Lecks and Mrs. Aleshine*, (52); Wallace, *Ben Hur*, (53); Richardson, *Clarissa*, (58); Rousseau, *Nouvelle Heloïse*,

How Old is Genius?

(50); Johnson, *Rasselas,* (50); Reade, *Griffith Gaunt,* (52).

In the sixties: Hugo, *Les Miserables,* (60); Butler, *The Way of All Flesh,* (66); Voltaire, *Candide,* (65); De Morgan, *It Never Can Happen Again,* (69); Defoe, *Robinson Crusoe* (60); de Goncourt, *La Faustin,* (60); James, *The Golden Bowl,* (60).

It will be plain that in many instances earlier work by a given artist might be indicated as of equal fame or equal importance, but the debate here would be no better than that over the superior quality of later work. I skirt the philosophy leading straight to the conclusion that if works of art endured by technique alone, age would have a general advantage. Tradition recognizes increasing skill and diminishing enthusiasm, and the artist who holds his high spirits—like a Goethe, a Verdi or a Cervantes—is yielded an inevitable ascendancy in art as in life.

My list is too personal and impulsive to merit precise deductions. It would not do, for example, to suggest that forty-two, fifty and sixty seem to be fortunate ages. It might be rash to suggest that in the work of the fifties and sixties appears a fiber stronger than in that of the thirties and forties. To be honest, I believe nothing of the sort. The thing I do believe is that genius as exhibited in works of imagination has no favorite age, that the brain has no child-bearing period whose range it is possible to fix.

The one admonitory conclusion which I venture to derive from this glance at the figures is that youth need not be in a hurry. A joyous impatience, yes, but not a crippling anxiety to demonstrate. No time concessions to all that is outside. The true artist will not be a clock-watcher. He may sometimes beat the game as Doctor Johnson did with *Rasselas* because he needed the money (it is always a shocking discovery that few impulsions have been so provocative to genius as being hard up), but this will not be like feverishly fussing over proof that genius is on the job early—or that earliness is genius.

Four Men

FOUR MEN

THE BLIND GIANT

WHEN I saw the tall man coming forward on the
tree-lined road I should, doubtless, have forgotten
everything if I had not been warned, and have said,
"Good afternoon, Mr. Pulitzer!" But the shorter man,
close at the elbow of the towering figure, lifted a finger to his lips. I was not to halt or speak; and I
watched the face move past, upturned in the darkness
of that bright day.

I had seen the chief in the morning at the Jekyl
Island villa, and was to meet him again on the morrow.
This particular hour of the afternoon belonged to the
interval in which certain theories were to be documented by the visitor for presentation at the next meeting. I was still a bit dazed by the impact of the
morning. When Joseph Pulitzer summoned one of
his editors that editor was to go prepared; but it was
part of the ordeal to discover that the test transcended
the lines of possible defense. It was as if you had
crammed for an examination in chemistry and the pro-

149

fessor had lightly chosen to consider your familiarity with the Rig Veda. At the very best a revelation of your collateral ignorances was a feature of the discipline. One emerged with a chastened feeling. Yet at that moment I had no sense of having seen the schoolmaster go by. The lanky giant with the chin like Lincoln's had freshly fascinated me.

In his brilliant biography of Joseph Pulitzer, Mr. Seitz emphasizes the fact that it was the editorial page which held Mr. Pulitzer's first and fiercest interest. Theoretically a mere Sunday editor did not need the intensive correction lavished upon one who wrote leaders, yet a Sunday editor who presumed upon such a theory was doomed to discomfort. All presumptions fell under the same hazard. Personal experiences might vary, Mr. Pulitzer's special intentions might vary, but the common result was of having any conceit vigorously if not violently ascertained, perhaps even extracted. If suspicion of this made a man more than cautious, if it diminished his confidence, he was no better off. Needless to say, this dynamic master was not looking for meekness. The marvel was in his instinct for hitting the weak spot. You were worthless if you were not sure, but it was useful that your sureness should have a little to go on, and at best your confidence needed to be qualified. Thus he asked me one day—casually, like a suave cross-examiner, "What was the Sunday circulation of the *World* week before last?" I could not tell him.

"Good God!" he threw up his arms in horror. "You don't know the circulation figures of your own paper! This is unthinkable—absolutely unthinkable! You *astound* me!"

It might seem eccentric, I said, but I had been too busy making the figures move to notice just what they were. All I knew definitely, was that the figures had been rising steadily since I had been made Sunday editor.

"That," he exclaimed with a withering inflection, "is mere arrogance, and I may remark to you that arrogance is an imperfect substitute for plain judgment. How can you judge of the reactions unless you watch the barometer of circulation? A knowledge of those figures is not merely a sordid obligation. It belongs to the integrity of your job. Reactions. You can't look your audience in the eyes, yet you must know about the response. These figures are your indication. How can you ignore response, or failures in response? Really, this is pathetic. Why, Morrel Goddard used to reach for the phone before he got out of bed on Sunday morning, to find out about the circulation figures."

Four Men

My defense was that I had been assured of the steady growth in circulation, that I always heard the figures and immediately forgot them. (He gasped hopelessly.) Moreover, as a person of some experience on the platform, it was enough for me to know that the crowd was increasing joyously. Numbers as arithmetic and numbers as a human inspiration had a relationship, but it seemed to me to make a big difference which you thought of in the midst of being an entertainer.

"Pitiful!" he growled. "A pitiful sophistry to cover a negligence—I won't say an indifference. When you look at a clock it isn't stultifying to notice the actual time."

I promised always to know precisely the figures of circulation, though I could not promise that these, as figures, would profitably influence my imagination.

"Imagination! I know what you mean by imagination—that it is necessarily inexact and irresponsible. I hope you will recover from that. I don't pick you out as an atrocious example—though I may be over indulgent. The truth is that too many newspaper men make the mistake many other people make about imagination. Imagination isn't distortion or sloppiness or substituting misinformation for something that should have been definitely ascertained. It isn't calling a thing

a holocaust that is only a fire, or describing a man as a
millionaire when he is worth a little money.   It isn't
being lazy or indifferent or lacking personal or professional conscience.   No.   It is what the astronomer
has when he says that right there, though no one has
yet located it, must be a star.   It is what Darwin had
when, with the long orchid in his hand, he said that
somewhere they would find the long-tongued moth
who visited it.   It is what the newspaper genius has
when he says that somewhere in Hell's Kitchen there
is a bartender who will tell the real story of a New
York Saturday night.   In other words, my friend,
imagination for the newspaper man is an *applied*
gift.   In him it is *the faculty for finding the fact."*

The vehemence, enormously kindling, with which
this admonition was thrown out, repeated itself vari-
ously in many another citation.   To give himself con-
crete illustration Mr. Pulitzer liked to ask what
suggestions for Sunday features I had found in that
morning's papers.   Sometimes the comment came in
a single word.   "Good!" or "Fantastic," or "Disagreeable."   Sometimes he chuckled and rebuked in response
to the same thing, the criticism breaking through the
grin.   "Oh, hold on, Black!   You're getting pretty
wild in that.   Ingenious—yes.   You were almost
splendid there, for a moment.   But rather silly too.

A little flighty. In the clouds. Come down. It isn't enough to be telling the truth. It must be *evident* that you are telling the truth. Remember that we're talking about a newspaper and not a romance."

This reminds me that he was deeply engaged by H. G. Wells' *The Time Machine* and *The War of the Worlds,* as well as by *A Modern Utopia,* then the most recent production of a restless imagination that always intrigued him. It was upon his suggestion that I spent a crowded hour with Wells at the Murray Hill Hotel, but neither this nor later meetings elicited from Wells the wished-for series of papers in the field of romantic fantasy. Wells was then incubating *New Worlds for Old,* and it was socialistic speculation that held his imagination. Yet the interviews, as such, were not unfruitful. I had met no other Englishman who talked so well; by which I mean that he was spontaneously easy. An English enemy might have called him glib. An American could scarcely fail to find him extraordinarily stimulating. Mr. Zangwill's later (much later) allusion to his audacious fertility had exemplification in his talk, which was, by what amounts to a paradox, as ready as his writing.

I liked to fancy a session between Wells and Pulitzer. It would have been a beautiful scrimmage. When it had ceased to be polite, what a spectacle to see the

two torrents meet, head on! Yet the theory may be
wrong. Mr. Pulitzer could step like a courtier when
he chose, and might have preferred elicitation to com-
bat. He never was pugnacious, even in irritable moments. His summing up could be superb, but his
master strokes were in cross-examination.

Naturally some such complacent conclusion occurs
to one who suffered the ordeal. Yet a false impression might result from forgetting the humor and the
free confessions of pleasure. His laugh was un-
grudging. And he could check this to place a correct-
ing foot-note, as when I quoted something and he said,
"No. Not Mark Twain. It was Lincoln." His
memory was staggering.

Certain of his newspaper prejudices opened the
way to lively argument. For example, he who had established the system of a right-hand position for the
leading news story on the first page of the morning
paper, so that the text might turn the sheet without
interruption, was profoundly opposed to a corresponding practise in the Sunday magazine. He wanted the
first page of the magazine to be complete in itself, despite the fact that a large picture in colors was an inevitable element of the page and that the text space
was thereby so restricted as to make the "turn over"
especially needful. On the last day of my visit to Jekyl

Island, he took up a criticism made with regard to a first-page feature. I was accused by an unnamed commentator of having shown Alice Roosevelt as received with royal honors in a presentation at the English court. With the sheet before him there was dramatic pathos in the fact that he, the presiding judge in the supreme tribunal, could not see the testimony. He called other eyes that were not those of the accused. Butes, Mr. Pulitzer's English secretary, was present and answered categorically, as the questions fell. How was Alice Roosevelt dressed in the picture? As all ladies dress who are presented at court. Were the appointments of the scene otherwise than those of a conventional presentation? They were.

"Then you have been stupidly criticized," said the chief. But it occurred to him completely to verify the integrity of the feature. Butes was to read the text. This also withstood analysis. But Mr. Pulitzer's supersensitive ears—the ears that had imposed astounding precautions against noise in the architecture of houses and ships—detected a suspicious crinkling, and he made a gesture of tragic grief.

"Does the story turn the page?"

"Yes," admitted Butes.

"This," cried the somber voice, as if pronouncing doom, "is a crime!"

Four Men

At that juncture, as if by a Belasco trick, the major-domo at the door spoke crisply. "Mr. Black must go, sir!"

It was the appointed time of departure in the motor-boat that would meet the north-going train.

"Mr. Pulitzer," I said, "isn't it possible that you might soften that phrase? It must be plain to you that I couldn't leave on the word 'crime.' "

"I'll do better. I not only soften it, I expunge it altogether."

He ran those long nervous fingers through my hair. "I should have left myself time to give more attention to your head. A fine head. Really, you have some astonishing bumps."

The protest that he had administered most of these drew a frankly forgiving laugh.

"Thank God! A good-natured man. There are too few of them. I must see you oftener. Good-by!"

Chugging through the twilight toward the Georgia coast, I was piercingly conscious of the looming world figure, now blazing, now stilled to the gentleness of a fine affection. It did not come into my thought that I should never see that great figure again. At a later time, I was to be the occasion of one of the sharpest annoyances of his life. But he could not take back the benediction. And if, in another world, he has, with

157

leisure for the little, chanced to come upon the real truth about his Sunday editor of that day, it may be that he would not wish to do so.

THE FRIEND

In one of the most charming volumes of reminiscence ever written by an actor, Otis Skinner speaks of his brother Charles with a fervor that expresses, in itself, a kind of happy fame. To the general reader it may well look like a graciousness of providence that one brother should be privileged, and should choose, to speak of another brother in terms of such devout acknowledgment. To a fellow sojourner who, also, came to feel a younger brother relationship with the same beautiful spirit, the tribute has a special music. By this guide, Otis Skinner tells us, he was made acquainted with the stars and first looked far into the other sky of books. I knew that voice and its evocations. I had the luck to come under the liberating spell of that enchanter, to be loosed by him into the secret places of Nature, the sacristies of art, and the whispering gallery of great men. When the world has quarreled its last quarrel, has reached the utmost mitigations for the problem of being born, it still will be true that the best of all possible educations begins with finding the right friend.

Four Men

I first saw C. M. S. on Brooklyn's Broadway, striding as one might who was by way of writing word-symphonies about the art of walking—his own walk was never less than *scherzo*. In *With Feet to the Earth* he mentions mischievously a family tradition that left him free to believe there might have been an Indian ancestor. He caught up this tradition when he leaped away from the town, and perhaps never quite shed it even in a crowded street. It was a tradition useful to a man who wanted leg liberty and a privilege of contempt for flummery. Country people who saw him shed his shoes had feelings of their own. He chuckled over that too.

On Brooklyn's Broadway he used to look to me like a hero. The black mustache, the black sombrero, the fluttering tie, all betokened the romantic. I wondered who he was. My boy imagination followed him longingly. Then, when I became the newest kid reporter on the *Brooklyn Times,* and took my place one day before the long black walnut copy table, there he was at my elbow. Happy omen! Veritably, reporting had opened the gate of romance. Beyond that gate my adventures took a glittering turn. Skinner was the conjurer. He wanted to write. He wanted to paint. He wanted to be a musician. He wanted to be a doctor. He did begin studies at the Long Island

Four Men

College Hospital and had a scalpel and carried home, across the Wallabout flats, fragments of the namelessly dead to be dissected in a hall room at midnight. But the blasphemous city editor learned his secret and adjusted assignments to defeat him. Moreover, he would be very hungry, for space rates were low and a medical education, even when you had a drag, came high. You could not count definitely, at any given time, upon assignment to a banquet. There was no nourishment in a lecture. A political meeting back of a barroom meant only a drink. Church fairs were often simply hungering. Police courts owned a smell that should have rebuked appetite, but youth has a forgiving nose. C. M. S. never ate inordinately. In the presence of the actual sacrament, there was about him, indeed, something of the exquisite. But he had an imagination for food. He could invest a prospective meal with a magnificence before which ordinary poetry failed. He was a Savarin of appreciation. When he dramatized a sixty-cent *table d'hôte* it expanded to regal dimensions. He was the impressario, he was the chef, he was the laureate. Gazing at an included glass of "red ink," he could give one the true feel of a *fiesta*, of some spectacular orgy, vast and foreign. Through the smoke of a five-cent cigar loomed a realized fantasy, with an oriental setting, gorgeous, glamourous and literary.

Four Men

We of the newspaper crowd, it may be remarked, made capital of his gourmet instincts. Thus when we acted *Our Boarding-House* for a charity (it was the audience that expressed the supreme benevolence) and Skinner was cast for the villain Fioretti, a plot was hatched for his discomfiture. A local caterer (paid by a line on the program) furnished authentic food for the stage dinner table. There could be no assumption that much would actually be eaten under the strain of watching for cues, and Skinner was most audibly enthusiastic over the prospect of a proper banqueting immediately after the final curtain. Since I, as the detective, was to handcuff him in the climax of the last scene, an opportunity for a sarcastic crisis transcending all stagey devices was offered by the privilege of losing the key to the handcuffs. Through the muted din of the last applause Skinner could be heard shouting, "Unlock them! Unlock them!" When the entire cast broke ranks for the banquet the painted villain grew imperative. *"Where's the key?"* No one seemed to know. Then came the deep chuckle that forgave every joke, and I saw the manacled hands flickering over the food. The perfect picture was of our handsomest intellectual, our undefeated epicure, in possession of a chicken leg and a mighty stalk of celery, the steel clicking at his wrists, and a grin, as of a tipsy calif, publishing his triumph.

Four Men

C. M. S. had to give up trying to be a doctor. He kept the scalpel for sharpening his pencil at Walt Whitman's desk in the old Williamsburg news shop.

He was left-handed and wrote a large, clear, copybook script. His formal manuscripts in ink (before the days of the typewriter) looked so much like those of an adolescent who had just mastered the pen that one could not but suspect a handicap in his bombardment of the magazines. Surely the optical effect of a grammar-school composition would interpose an unfortunate impression. With one hand upon a heap of rejected treasures, he would overhaul his change pocket and thrust out one foot. "Behold the artist's fate! Thirty cents and a busted shoe!" He insisted, at this juncture, that he possessed a gift for always having exactly thirty cents.

Then the magazines began to "get" him. His happy books, *Do-Nothing-Days*, *Nature in a City Yard*, *Little Gardens* and *American Myths and Legends*, included papers that received a cordial welcome in the *Century* and elsewhere. His earlier work reflected the influence of Emerson and Thoreau. (It awed me that he had once shaken hands with Emerson on a Rhode Island train.) The pungent rebel of Walden Pond had lured him strongly. Himself of New England, and accepting the outdoor traditions of the Concord region,

he liked to array himself with Thoreau as a wayward
son. Perhaps he was a kind of city Thoreau. The
rebellions were, of course, chiefly literary, though he
was ever a lusty individualist. In his later work, when
he had found himself and a terse, lucid and graphic
style, he attained a delightful blend of aphoristic
humor, freshness of description and forthright charm.

Meanwhile we had roamed together and sailed together (in a temperamental catboat) over the regions
adjacent to New York. He was an appalling walker.
As a plain walker I often felt as if sacrificed to a
theory. That deep chuckle came as reward enough for
the pun that the one with the shorter legs was slaugh-
tered to make a roaming holiday. Yet he could dally
with superb indifference to time or destination. Finding rare ferns or bits of quartz on the Palisades filled
him with real excitement. He could give an epic
glamour to geology. A new subtlety in syringas burst
upon him like an apocalypse. Any astonishing thing
might happen in this game Nature was playing. Evolution, as the supreme drama, was always springing sur-
prises. It kept you breathless. He would have had
a grin when he wrote in one of his essays that much
may be made of the oyster when it has been to college.

They established him as critic of art and music.
He took me with him to the studios and exhibitions.

Four Men

Before and after he found shelter under the wings of the *Brooklyn Eagle* he wrote of art with consummate discernment and beauty. Certainly he was one of the best music critics of his time. His own touch at the piano was eerie and exquisite. Without dexterity, he had an unfailing sense of tone color, the absence of which no mere finger facility ever is able to hide, and gave the orchestra-sound to the simplest harmonics. In Heller or Grieg he could vent that gnomish quaintness he had, while in passages out of Wagner came a mounting magic as of string tracery with the cool shadows of the wood and the blood red of brass. There was something fragile, though not brittle, in his playing, a kind of disembodied emotionalism, as of a soul plucking at winds, at the shaggy hair of hilltops, at grasses in the sun. It was by his inspiration that I first sought to master the *Traumerei*. Quite naturally this echoed his version.

Then, in his prime, out of a fragrant home, with two fine sons prospering, and the wife-who-understood beside him, they carried C. M. S. up to Vermont to die. The operation told him, as it told us, that he had but a little while. Propped in the bed he could see the cedars and a roll of hills. "What luck!" he said, waving a hand toward the revealing window. "Think of having a view like that!" He meant, to die with.

Four Men

A little group of friends who must presently go back to New York hovered miserably in the old parlor with its ancestral trophies. Word came through that C. M. S. had heard no music for a long time, and would I play the *Traumerei*. I sat at the piano, blinded by tears. Nothing could have seemed more completely impossible than playing six intelligible notes. I could not feel hands or keys. The room swirled. Yet I might live a long life and never again hear in any single moment so high a call for the utmost effort. The man to whom music was a religion, whose splendid brow had been bathed by the symphonies of the masters, who had, for me, opened the door to divinity, was lying alone waiting for the last earthly chords he was likely to hear. I prayed my way through the little piece, in a kind of exultant agony. God knows what the sounds were. It should have been enough that Charlie, in that parting minute, muttered, "Old man, it went right to the spot!"

In a few weeks . . . "with feet to the earth" . . . amid the hills.

THE MAN WHO WAS ALONE

Only an editor, perhaps, may apprehend certain sorts of heroism. Only he may sense in the ink stains the not quite hidden implications of life-blood, or suspect the grim fortitudes behind sheets of spotless copy. Better than many another he may know how seldom the real heroes and the real heroines reach the turn in the path that may come under the arbitrary spotlight of fame.

Unfortunately for himself, the editor never is able to detach from his celebrities the color of their collateral traits. Thus I always find myself thinking of O. Henry as vividly late. Worse than that, any story of his, even one that never came under my hand and that should, in all decency, hold a presumption of innocence until proved guilty, somehow acquires a look of having been born after it was due. This is an inexcusable attitude. The travail of the parent is no part of the child's sins. Yet I can fancy a midwife's feelings before the brood of a mother who always had a hard time. Even a kind of accusatory bitterness might creep in.

The truth is that I became accustomed, week in and week out, to the likelihood of receiving O. Henry's stories, short as they were, in propitiatory fragments; sometimes in two pieces, sometimes in three. Those that came complete made no deepness of impression for that circumstance. Thus are our virtues taken for granted and our defects hailed as a habit. (Moreover, there was the accusatory contrast of other contributors.

Zona Gale or Irvin Cobb, for example, were more professionally reasonable.) The coming of the first fragment of an O. Henry story acknowledged the reasonableness of my official anxiety, for the weekly stories in the *World* had to be illustrated, and the illustrations needed a little information about scene and characters. Often this preliminary part (on the last day of grace) held no adequate hint for the draughtsman, but an accompanying line would wig-wag: "The picture might be of a traffic cop holding open a pathway for a pretty girl."

The last fragment frequently had the effect, by its tardiness, of having been wrung from a tortured spirit. In most instances this was, doubtless, a fantastic illusion. Very commonplace circumstances of neglect, of miscalculation, of a counter-irritant, can explain and make familiar the failures in adjustment on the part of harried producers. But the panting arrival of the last part provoked editorial speculation as to whether his "stinger" at the end had not given O. H. a bit of trouble. Did he prophesy the formula of the short-story courses in which he is blandly used as a model and have his "stinger" ready when he began? Or was the "O. Henry finish" a deferred obligation chucked into the hands of Chance, and creating, quite often, the annoyances of a promissory note? I am not con-

cerned with the horrors of formulæ or with the fact
that an O. Henry story is the worst of all possible
models for the uninspired tinkerer, but with the strictly
human implications of his apparent wrestlings.
Whether he had his finish ready and was bothered on
the journey to meet it; whether he found excitement
in devising it when its time came; or whether an inertia, such as could hold him on a park bench for hours
at a stretch, gives the simplest and most conclusive explanation, are subtleties that did not soften the distresses of those who waited.

The offender could awake to sparkling excuses.
Sometimes these were not more original than those
offered by an office boy with his eye on a ball game.
Again, they would be ingenious. Always they would
be joyously colloquial. Promises had a like flavor.
"You can bet your variegated socks that I will send you
an Easter story," was typical. Or the reassurance
might run (as it did in 1907), "May the ink in my
bottle turn to Old Crow on the day that I hesitate to
use it at the desire of you and the still dear World."
My confrère of those days, Mr. William Johnston,
(who received the impact of many of the excuses) has
quoted Porter's rejoinder to the declaration of a certain magazine editor that the situation really warranted
the kicking of the culprit. Porter replied cheerily that

he never would be found so tardy in the matter of any obligation that could be fulfilled with the feet.

That interesting reportorial go-between, Bill Williams—it was he who executed the details of a search that brought O. Henry and the *World* together—may some day give a wholly satisfying characterization of Sydney Porter as a man. If Williams could sit as he did, hour after hour, in the room where Porter was writing, knowing by some miracle, the rare art of inoffensive silence, he must have attained a relationship that understood. It is clear that Williams never sought to elicit confidences. Evidently he exercised precisely the right sort of discretion. Beyond all that, he must have proved to be the one kind of company possible of election to a contact which any writing person will be ready to regard as especially delicate; so that the intimacy doubtless derived neither from philosophy nor from conscious conduct. Each was able to be himself without offense to the other; which, when they had discovered it, would make for comfort. In their night walks the two seem to have been richly mute for long spaces. Tennyson and Carlyle had no more eloquently speechless intervals. Their friendship jogged along. To each the other simply *was,* or I deduce that much from the way in which Williams emerged, without theories, without analytical luggage, and without testimony indicating any meagerest intrusion on O. Henry's part. To Williams there had remained scarcely less than the general sense of mystery as to Porter. No allusions to himself, to his affairs of the moment, to his history, had the effect of greatly diminishing one's feeling of Porter's inscrutable strangeness. Beyond any reticence that was to be accounted for by his history, there was an oddly tentative effect in his associations. Not even Lafcadio Hearn had seemed to me more unadjustable. On certain occasions when I met Porter he would be as spontaneous as in his letters. Again he would have a sort of sagacious wistfulness. When he told me that a publisher had suggested putting together a volume of his stories, and that he would like, for such purpose, to make free of his contributions to the *World* (he had written considerably more than a hundred), his pleasure in the consent, yielded as a matter of course, was quite characteristically expressed in an impulse to be the superior giver.

"I'll write you a special story," he said, "and there'll be no bill for it." This bargain naturally was refused. The story would be welcome, but the check would go to him in the usual way. As for the privilege to put the stories in a book, it carried the *World's* blessing.

Four Men

Commonly he acted as a transient creature who had
dropped in upon civilization and who patiently and un-
critically endured the awkwardness. With one, or with
two, whom he found colloquially easy, he might give
no such sign for the duration of a chumming period.
In an office, in any set situation, in whatsoever group
that involved more than an elemental comradeship, he
was wary if not restless. One who sought to explain
him by his product might have fancied the persistent
lure of story-making places, by the suggestive atmosphere of queer streets and of shabby squares with their
shifting population of bench loungers. It pleases the
amateur in psychology to think of story-writers as
"looking for material." O. Henry was a lonely figure
by no fanatic search for plot dressings. The beggar
upon whom he thrust a five-dollar bill was not challenged for any tale of misadventure. He could not be
imagined as a cross-examiner. Perhaps he would have
felt fearful of spoiling a better story already in his
head.

One day he was persuaded to join a party of newspaper artists and writers who were to make holiday at
a little Long Island picnic park. The word picnic suggests the youth of the earth, and this enterprise was,
indeed, happily juvenile. Perhaps professional gaiety
was then more innocent. Certainly it was more primitive. There was to be a forty-yard dash in which the

fat and the lean would suffer their appointed humiliations. The day began with a noontime feast, served (or acquired) at a long board. O. Henry, sitting opposite, afforded close opportunity for speculation. How would he unfold in the frivolities of the day? To the brutal banter he gave oblique appraisal. Evidently the jollity pleased him. He bore his share of notice. There was a low-voiced participation when this was imposed. Probably it occurred to more than one that it would be novel to watch him emerge at last from his diffidence. Yet I knew that even there, in the midst of the hubbub, he was alone. He was always alone. It occurred to me that it was this faculty for being alone that had made it possible for him to write with Williams in the room.

Then he disappeared. It may have happened when we left the table to spill into the quaint acre. At all events, "Where is O. Henry?" had no answer. He had utterly gone.

When I saw him, a week or so later, not without an anxiety that had considered the possible roughness of our group and its effect upon him, he gave no first sign of having to give account, and seemed sharply caught up by my mild inquiry. The truth is that I at once felt guilty of a supplementary brutality in sight of his suddenly kindled embarrassment.

"You know," he said, "I found a wonderful road."
This was all. It would have been cruel and fruit-
less to ask farther.

He always was finding wonderful roads—one-man
roads. The road might have the length of an alley.
It might run through a desert or quiver with tawdry
lights. When he was alone he understood them. Maybe he was like an electric needle that points true when
there is no other steel near it. Too soon he went forth
on the dark path which every man must travel alone.

THE KING IN WHITE

If I had escaped a little sooner from the thrall of
the New England literary oligarchy I might have done
better in that first visit to William Dean Howells. It
is true that no guest could have been treated with a
simpler kindness. But Howells had been the intimate
of the elect. The imagination of a pre-Freudian novice
saw him as wearing the robes of a *noblesse*. His
gracious lightness served only to emphasize the back-
ground turrets of tradition.

For one thing, that fine head, set so strongly upon
an uncommonly short neck, was more familiar in print
than any other of the time, save perhaps, those of
Longfellow and Mark Twain. There is, to the young,

a mesmeric influence in such reiterated presentments. Though Howell's portraits gave him an effect of contemplative vigor, he appeared to me, in the flesh, as more rugged than I had fancied. I experienced a like effect some years later, in meeting James Russell Lowell, when the surprise of the reddish tinge in his beard was part of the discovery that the literary portraits had been sweetened. Howells gave one a sense of directness that discriminated, of a fastidious forcefulness, ripe and sure, yet neither constrained nor offish.

In that day, of the late 'eighties, I was writing a first book, a story-history of Ohio, and privileged information about a certain Martin's Ferry boyhood acquired a luminous importance. Yet the book, and the needful data, solemnly as I regarded these, were not my whole concern. Here was Howells, at last, seated accessibly in his study on Central Park South, and making his visitor as comfortable as he could. Ohio was all right, but this opportunity looked larger than any state. It was too bad that all the things I wanted to ask him about novel-writing seemed so hard to get into words. If only he might have become garrulous! As I was to learn afterward, he could be keener to ascertain an interviewer than to reveal himself. A newspaper man, talking to one who had been a newspaper man, ought to have been able to do better. The trouble lay in the miserable awe; and it may be that I was hampered a good deal by the very definiteness of an alarm-clock resolution to ask a certain question which I had brought with me, like a terrier on a string, and which had been rubbing against the legs of my thought from the moment I came in. What else *could* any one heatedly wish to ask Howells? Wasn't it the one question about him that persisted in not being answered? And here was the man himself, like a witness in the dock. . . .

Why, I wanted to know, did Howells ignore the sordid in life? Why did the man who welcomed Tolstoy and the other Russians who, critically, was so indubitably a democrat, with so alert a sympathy for every phase of strivings toward a better social order, persistently avoid, in his own art, the element of tragedy.

When the thing had been said, desperately, with the sound of a detached and inexcusable impudence, I was stabbed by remorse. The regret was not theoretical. I could see reason for regret in the fading urbanity of his look. Perhaps it was only the twinge of boredom, though the effect seemed deeper. Perhaps his thought had muttered, "Good God—*again!*" A thousand reviewers had challenged or extenuated the trait of avoidance. Fiske and James and Hale and Alden and all the rest would each have found a way of asking the same thing, or doing worse by being decent as in the presence of an infirmity. And here was a stripling with the silly platitude, wanting to know . . .

"Tragedy?" he repeated, without sharpness, yet with a trace of the acid that might have been spilled by a reminiscent annoyance. "Don't you think there was something of the tragic in Bartley Hubbard before the divorce court?"

I am sure that at once he was sorry, sorry to have been tripped into a defensive citation. My admission that Bartley *was* tragic mended nothing. There could be no debate that would not be absurd. An artist may not explain himself. He must be taken as he happens. He must take himself as he happens. So far as my question is concerned I might as well have asked him why he brushed his hair forward or wore a mustache. If I had been old enough I might have been aware that any man's theory of his own work is no better than his theory of himself, which never can be more than questionably contributory to a judgment. What a man calls his principles are but a kind of firm name for his instincts. Howells' avoidances were not philosophic. They were temperamental; which is to say that they were, in him, not avoidances at all. The artist, too, may like what he likes. Though Howells did cite one of the very few sordidly tragic situations in all his fiction, this unconsidered retort was a mere argumentative reaction. His considered argument would have been that each of us has abysses of drama, that the most scathing action can be in the clash of thoughts and words. Mature judgments may see this as implicit in all of his work. He could appreciate Gogol and be Howells. Our rich heritage from him testifies to the selective consistency that gives any art its coherence.

Critically Howells insisted that the instincts should act honestly. Thus, he gave a hearty welcome to my friend Henry Harland's *Yoke of the Thorah.* But Harland's later period of London and the Yellow Book seemed to him meretricious, and *The Cardinal's Snuffbox* as a less honest performance. Romance or realism might remain an open question, but Howells wanted a realistic brand of integrity.

Under the circumstances the sight of Howells in the audience at the *première* of my first picture play, *Miss Jerry,* in 1894, made me apprehensive. (On another occasion it was Howells and Brander Mathews, sitting side by side.) It is one thing to hide in the wings at one's play. It was quite another to speak an opening part in person, then stand in the dark and talk for all of one's characters—this being the innocent form of the screen drama I had devised in those days before the motion picture.

In his letter saying that he liked the story he added: "The invention is novel and agreeable and delightfully surprising. As an elderly New Yorkized Bostonian, going on fifty-eight, I found it a little long [the first showing ran mercilessly for two hours] but if I had been a young man, listening and looking with some young girl I had brought with me, I should have wished it to go on forever. You have struck boldly at life in your story, and you have got a fresh note from it. Memnon always sings to the rising sun, you know." Perhaps my best compliment for the picture plays, not excepting Grover Cleveland's interest, was Howell's second coming, this time at another private showing in J. Wells Champney's studio a few weeks later, when his daughter became the "young girl I had brought with me."

Twenty-five years passed before I talked with Howells again, this time at the St. Hubert on Fifty-seventh Street. I heard him at the seventy-fifth birthday dinner when George Harvey of Harper's presided, with President Taft at the board—and, for a man who loathed public speaking, he made an astonishly good speech. I shall mention the circumstances of a last meeting not only because ego is indispensable to reminiscence, but because it is only thereby that I may show that one may, in a single lifetime, enjoy the true feel of a reincarnation. Having reviewed *The Great Desire,* Howells expressed to the publishers a wish that he might meet the author. The meeting, not less than the terms of the wish, indicated that he had quite forgotten all earlier contacts, so that I was welcome to the emotion of being a new person, which soon had a way of not seeming altogether honest. Yet he was not to be induced to go back and gather up anything. He wanted to know how I came to write the book. Upon my side were acute curiosities about him. We seesawed at interrogation. Under such circumstances there could be little flow. It was my confession of a double life, as editor for the great audience and as writer for the small one, that incited the counter-confession not to be had by conscious method or intention. He too had been editor and novelist at the same time. And it had been a prodigious drudgery. By contract he was editor of the *Atlantic* and producer of a novel a year. It was to be seen that he looked back upon these conditions with a kind of mellowed indignation, particularly as upon an incredible *tour de force* in patience, since a small salary was accompanied by an employing expectation that the thing might go on indefinitely. Breaking away, coming to New York and easier conditions, (including the Easy Chair of *Harper's*), had made life for him a different affair.

Suddenly he fixed me with an intent look, "You know New York. That is evident in every page."

"From you," I began, "who have been here a quarter of a century—"

"Ah, yes!" he exclaimed, dismissing any homage I might have offered, "but I was nearing sixty when I came! You are native."

It did not push aside something that was in his mind to protest that mere scene was a secondary matter, perhaps much less important than might be indicated by the word secondary.

"I don't mean the mere scene," he said. "I mean the place-spirit—that ruling denominator of the diversity . . ."

There was excuse for mentioning that "NewYorkized" in his old letter, and for insisting that if no place could really "ize" him it was because the American spirit was his concern, and because the great scene for every artist is the scene inside himself.

He nodded. "I know the kindly thing you want to say. Of course you are right enough about the scene inside. I suppose it is determinative. Yet—"

He did not tell me what he was thinking. He who had been in the Middle West of his boyhood, in the New England of his prime, in the New York of his full maturity, was, perhaps, relating all, for the moment, to those unanswered and wholly individual questionings that must come to every artist. He who could "embrace the common" and "sit at the feet of the familiar," who could resist, with apparent serenity (though it was emphatically not that) all temptation to be different, and who could, to the end, with the meticulous integrity of a Meissonier, objectify details of the human drama, as he saw it, in his elected field and in himself, hovered there like a brooding king who had found that life was larger than empire. This effect, vivid as it was, betokened a much deeper characteristic discerned by every intimate, and not to be bidden from any one privileged to associate the image of the man with the lineaments of his work. Howells' philosophy, his religion as an artist, was that somehow from the complexity of the simple would be elicited the ultimate truth about the whole. Raucous and dirty things also are true, as he was ready to admit; but if a picture of a society may be constructed from study of its diseases, the implication is that a picture quite as authentic may be built from study of its norm. Howells, however, was not separated and distinguished simply by hating to handle the pathological. It was his temperamental repugnance, as a writer, toward stuff that would be hot in the mouth (as he once put it) that presented the really ineradicable difference.

Four Men

Thus, only as a producer was he a specialist, and only in art is specialization subject to abuse. Already it begins to appear that he will be elaborately misunderstood, but also it is apparent that valid criticism may recognize him as perhaps supremely the interpreter of his time.

The Waiter Complex

THE WAITER COMPLEX

THE lawyer stood before the jury box with the little board in his hands, a slotted board suggesting one of those devices for railroad-train chess or solitaire, in which were slips of paper naming the possible jurors. He had a gracious air that did not fit him. There was in his look something disenchanted, if not a fixed expectation of impending bitterness. This amiability in his battling face meant that I might be accepted as a juror, in which event it would not do to have annoyed me. Yet it was necessary to find out whether I was fit. To do this without affront required a certain ingenuity which I contemplated with interest, and with a reserve of my own, for on that particular day there were reasons for regarding as a definite misfortune this demand to serve or save the state. The human experience of sitting on a jury was, in fact, alluring in itself; but this was not the day in which I could comfortably abandon myself to the enjoyment. So that you might say I was touchy.

The lawyer leaned forward, with a most unsatisfactory expression of solicitude, to ask me: "Have you any prejudice against the owners of motor trucks?"

The case was, indeed, one involving violent contact between a motor truck and a humbler vehicle drawn by a horse. Nothing could be more logical than the ascertaining of any possible antipathy to motor trucks as motor trucks.

"No," I said. "I have lost all my prejudices—all but one."

It was a foolish thing to say. How foolish, I began to see by a kind of kindled change in the face of the lawyer. The face became suddenly normal. Moreover, the judge who had been woodenly withdrawn, with the glaze of boredom in his eyes, sat sharply forward and cupped a hand against his good ear. He seemed to know that the lawyer would not let it go at that.

"Eh—," stammered the lawyer, leaning still farther forward, with an eager respectfulness, but not, you may be sure, without sign of a malicious curiosity that was made more appalling by the dramatic quiet of the court room, "if it may not be considered impertinent, might I ask you to tell us the subject of your last surviving prejudice?"

"Waiters," I said.

While the judge sat back and undulated silently,

the lawyer, with a most illegal grin, made something like a bow, to be divided, evidently, between me and the bench, and remarked, "I scarcely need to say that your single prejudice does not appear to the prosecution as at all disqualifying."

I was accepted. Both lawyers accepted me. One might have deduced from the suddenness that if you are immaterial and irrelevant enough your chances of escaping a jury box are specifically reduced. Also it might indicate any number of things as to having a wrong prejudice in a right place. Any prejudice is an infirmity, but an infirmity has its relativities. A prejudice as to something else may even suggest that you will be especially amenable as to the matter in hand.

In court there would be no debate as to a prejudice bearing directly upon the matter in hand. On the printed page the situation must be somewhat different. And a preliminary confession should have enormous weight. Moreover, my prejudice against waiters is not one of those blind aversions that must always be distasteful to the civilized. It is a prejudice established on large lines, a mellow and philosophical prejudice. Standing alone, it is, perhaps, one that should not be made less secure. I can not but feel that a person without at least one prejudice would be open to special suspicion.

The Waiter Complex

Speaking thus, with my prejudice gathered about me, in neat folds, if not as with a privileged toga at least with the manner of one who wears all that he has handy, I may urge the point that this prejudice should not demand explanation. The fact that it hangs so discordantly in the spiritual wardrobe of an otherwise amiable disposition should show that it is not characteristic. If it is not characteristic, if each of us requires one dissonance, it does not need excuse. And if it is excusable why analyze it? One might be better occupied in analyzing waiters. No one has ever succeeded in such an effort. Everything else has been dissected to the bones. The waiter stands quite alone. I can imagine Analysis contemplating him, perhaps even coveting him, but turning away again and again, possibly with no logical reason but simply by some unnamable sense of futility. Theoretically you can split up the atom, and men have gone about that enterprise cheerfully. Taking the waiter apart . . . no. It can't be done. He is irreducible.

The waitress? Ah! that is another matter. I shall mention waitresses, but only as a distantly related species, and not at all in contradiction of my point that the waiter is a unique obstacle. And I must not let highly isolated individual instances disturb the rule. I have known waiters who were philosophers of a profound sort, men of evident learning, with faculties of discernment so penetrating that one stood (that is to say, sat) in awe of them. I have met waiters with an exalted sense of humor, with that flicker of fundamental wit which can illuminate the subtlest crevices of character. I have listened spellbound to raconteurs with burnsides and a delicious discretion who made ordinary talkers seem of a blundering ineptitude. These outstanding instances do not invalidate the type. The fact that a given waiter might be fit to preside over a presidential cabinet or any less submissive board of directors, that he might make you think of a disguised ambassador, or a prelate privately ascertaining certain facts about the so-called human race, can not upset my contention. I knew one waiter upon whom fell the suspicion of being a Roumanian prince in ingenious exile. He looked the part, and so nearly seemed to act it that one fumbled the dinner. Moreover, the looks of waiters can be a prodigious disturbance. How often has a certain waiter robbed every other male in his vicinage of any slightest effect of importance? The bad taste of having a serving person hit the lines of an ultimate distinction needs no remark. A reasonable handsomeness is well enough, but the principle of the thing is accented repeatedly by the comments women venture. A waiter who is ludicrously impressive can make a

woman an utterly inadequate dinner companion. And
this is not saying a word about the distractions inter-
posed by good looking very young waiters who excite
speculation as to whether they are otherwise college
boys and thus arouse among feminine spectators disproportionate sympathy.

Naturally the incidental waiter is excluded from
my prejudice. He is not a true waiter. Under the
simplest tests he would not show authentic reactions.
In fact, if you even think you understand him he is,
probably, a pretender. True waiters, I repeat, resist
the acid of analysis. Something happens to their
humanness when they become waiters. For this reason no possible testimony from any incidental incum-
bent is worth hearing. Even a reformed waiter would
be misleading. If he could reform he would be
counterfeit.

Being held to the consideration of external effects
we have to note that waiters present an immense
variety. They are not, to be sure, so varied as res-
taurants. They do nevertheless take on coloration.
Even a true waiter, perhaps especially a true waiter,
will synchronize with his surroundings. If it is a
noisy place he will, however regretfully, be noisy. A
symphonic waiter cast for the moment in a jazz situation will show his reservations, but art is art and
obligatory unisons will command him.

The Waiter Complex

The varieties I speak of are not fixed by colorations. A morose waiter is not morose because of surroundings. He might undertake to make you think so, or you might deduce that he was to be explained by the new chef, by his antipathy for the woman at the checking desk, or (logically) by prohibition. If you can thus be misled you are not equipped for the study. You must not do as people do about marriage, for example, or, for that matter, the income tax report. Charging every trait to overhead is an immoral trick. No marriage can be so bad as marriers may happen to be. Waiters, then, are humanly rather than professionally different. This ought to help analysis. By brushing aside the environment you should be able to come close to the truth about them. But it can't be done. Trying to get the waiter's character in focus is like trying to catch his eye. He sees all that he wishes to see, either through the front or the back of his head. Your lamb gets cold and you halt all dinner talk during an interval of wishing for him. In a common restaurant you can make an uproar. Where the surroundings reach a certain quality a crashing summons may not seem desirable. He takes advantage of this likelihood. Some joy as yet unanalyzed warms his aloofness—perhaps at a distance no greater than four paces.

Female waiters do not specialize so markedly in

aloofness. On the other hand you can not call them. You are able on shipboard to say, "Steward!" You may mutter "Waiter!" witheringly, or give any color you choose to "Garçon!" But one does not say "Waitress!" even in a place where she is likely to answer (when she hears you) "Yes, dearie!" However, her human habit of catching glances has a constant tendency to soften this profoundest irritation. Like a shopgirl she can have a passionate absorption in things she is not supposed to be doing, but she has not the deep hatred of response that wraps a male waiter in an impregnable aura.

Probably some instinct of escape is behind this waiter trait. He not only puts you in your place, not only proves that you are helpless without him, but leads you straight to the chagrin of suspecting that the whole miserable scheme of things by which there *are* waiters is one which you have criminally helped. You are flung into a dependent class. He seems to be enjoying a mute contempt, as who should say, "This dog should be waiting on *me!*" When he does accept the signal it may be with a feigned humility or with the lofty complacence of a presiding autocrat muttering, "The chair recognizes the gentleman from Georgia!" But he has made his point. You may have needed sugar or a spoon, yet before all you have needed *him*.

The Waiter Complex

Law is no better than the policeman. You must weigh the restaurant by the waiter; and that he should realize this during his long intervals of thought is explanation enough for any effect of lurking intention.

It would be a great mistake to forget that the waiter has codes. He would not descend to teaching, but his rebukes are educational, and I am sure it would not offend him to become conscious of this result. He knows that, save at breakfast, you should not want coffee until the end of the meal. If you ask for concurrent coffee he will use every evasion known to him, even to the extreme of an incredulous glare. Should he mildly like you he may only look hurt. You may see him wince as though stabbed to the quick. Coffee *with* . . . ! He hates to believe that he has heard aright. You need a keeper, or at least the whispered restraint of a firm friend. *Coffee!*—and otherwise you appear sane enough. Perhaps if he simply overlooks the blunder or (say) the absent-mindedness, the ends of mercy will be attained. If then you ask, "Where *is* the coffee?" you may see him totter away in rage or grief.

It is foolish of him to be sensitive about behavior, but even a specialist may have prejudices—perhaps only one, that may at certain moments acidulate an entire disposition. I can imagine a waiter who loves all mankind except when mankind is meeting one of the crises of essential sustenance. I can fancy him crying out, "O God!—if only they wouldn't *eat!*" If they didn't eat he couldn't be a waiter. Perhaps that is the point. It may be food that is making all the trouble in the world. Any book on proper food does more than raise the question. The way the world has been eating for millions of years explains everything. I met a charming man who warned me *never* to drink water. It was then April and he assured me that he had not tasted water since January. I met another who pleaded with me to *guzzle* water. If possible I was to wake up frequently in the night and drink water passionately. Both men, I believe, are still alive, which may prove that it is wrong for the waiter to have prejudices.

It is a mistake, evidently, to assume that the waiter's sensitiveness about the tip relates wholly to the matter of its size. Thanks for a small tip and silence for a large one upsets the vulgar theory. Neither sarcasm nor awe is a sufficient explanation. Theoretically his manner at the moment of the tip corresponds to the professor's mark on your examination paper. You may hope to stalk out with a C plus, proud of yourself. All this is illusory. He is actuated by something hidden. I suspect that you may buy a caricature of attention but that you can not buy his approval. Remember that he too has been reading Karl Marx, and that as a result he may feel himself to be the repository of the last embers—that he may regard himself as carrying the ultimate protest, mute but inextinguishable, against an absurd civilization. In this view he may have a kind of grandeur which, if you apprehend it, will hurt your digestion. This is the evil of the waiter. The emotion of eating should be splendidly single and his horribly artificial intrusion can pervert the poetry.

The flippant attitude of eaters who do not choose, or are organically unable, to consider these things, often embitters what should be a private festival. Waiters may be disconcerted, but they always win. The fearful weight of their traditions submerges the seated culprit. And in meek America the spectators always side with the waiter. This is particularly true in the case of a complaint. No trait is more distinctively American than that of regarding the kicker as a nuisance.

Thus, with the waiter on one hand and social pressure on the other, the eater is potently regulated when he faces, as it were, the cook. Speaking of social pressure, I recall an incident, or rather a pair of them, that may support me. (I am not quoting a good story, but simply reciting a typical personal experience.) In a western hotel dining hall administered by waitresses, a long table was surrounded by a heterogeneous group of men, most of them road salesmen,—as you would have said, with statistics to help your wild guess. One figure in the group was rotundly conspicuous. I remember thinking that he looked like Tom Reed, then Speaker of the House of Representatives. He was florid, slightly breathless and very genially audible.

With the bill of fare in his fat fist and the waitress hovering behind his chair, he inquired, absently, "My dear, do you think you could learn to love me?"

The table company was laced into a taut attention.

"I don't have to," answered the girl, quite as absently, "I do already."

A grin ran round the board. Only one cackle arose. It came from a lean, mincing man with a fragile upturned mustache, who continued for some moments to give the effect of saying, "That was a good one!"

The next day, at a not greatly different hotel, I found myself in another group of men whose disposition may not have been greatly different, though I suspect that they may have been assembled at a hungrier time of day or in worse weather. At all events there was a thick pall of silence spattered by crockery sounds and the clink of utensils, when I heard, piercingly, "My dear, do you think you could learn to love me?"

The Waiter Complex

It was that mincing little man with the mustache whom I instantly identified by a silly air of suspended experimentation. He had heard, the day before, what his foolish head measured as a good one. But this was the wrong place, the wrong time, the wrong girl, and he was very much the wrong man. He did not look ·fatly paternal, his voice had no jovial flavor. Anything he did was predestined to flatness. The drab young woman who awaited his order glared sullenly. He at once looked completely imbecile, shrinking in the silence like a torture-chamber culprit. There was indeed a kind of maudlin suspense broken at last by an old man at the far end of the table who grunted, "Rotten!"

It is, then, to be admitted that the waiter, of any sex, is held in place by the relentless mechanism of our civilization. Some people make a mess of trying to be brutal with waiters, perhaps on a conscientious theory of going after service—they thus expound it. Others yield to ridiculous familiarities. Only the perfectly bred—the trained stand patters—escape the itch to disturb that which can not be disturbed. If you have failed to be submissively bred, if you are unable to see in the waiter as a Figure, appointed and essential to the best of all possible worlds, you have but one alternative:

The Waiter Complex

Keep a prejudice. Stop haggling with your Unconscious, or arguing with ethics. Let your house-broken prejudice do the absolutely indispensable barking.

Meeting Authors

MEETING AUTHORS

It is said of a certain statue of Edwin Booth that on the day of its first appointed showing in New York a lady approached one of the members of the committee in a state of cultured indignation. "I suppose," she exclaimed, indicating the effigy, "it is all very well, *but these are not Mr. Booth's legs!*"

We may assume that the resulting discussion had points of delicacy for both parties, yet more important was the suggestion that intricate dangers are entailed by greatness. You never can tell to what lengths hero worship may go, into what subtleties it may descend. It is true that the legs of an actor are, in a manner of speaking, a public matter. The point is that worship can be analytical, and that while another sort of greatness might escape with its legs, it never can hope to enjoy an abstract homage. The worshiper *notices,* and in a sad number of cases the result is unfortunate both for the one who suffers observation and for the one who is thereby too much informed.

Hero worship is understood to be going out, but people still have acute curiosities which often look much like the same thing. And there are always those who refuse to know that a thing is passé. A new Peter Pan who should ask, "You *do* believe in heroes, don't you?" would elicit an astonishing chorus of sheepishly affirmative answers. The most we can be sure of is that hero-love, if not more fickle, now lacks the fiber of a steadfastness it used to have; or that something more perishable has crept into the quality of heroes. So that it never was more needful to issue a warning against personal meetings. If you value the nourishment of a happy illusion, keep your celebrity at long range.

My anxiety at the moment is the special danger of meeting authors. The nature of their work in the world is such that authors can not afford, we are told, to be public characters. Theoretically they ought, however moderately, to mix, but it is notorious that they usually fail at the job. Overwhelming testimony has made it plain that they are likely, in any social torture place, to be uninterestingly miserable, appallingly rude, or simply to have the effect of not coming off. There is no longer a certainty that they will merely be queer. Being merely that never was really calamitous. It could be a shock to have your mental picture contradicted, but one becomes accustomed to taking these shocks. With the meagerest experience one learns that

looking the way they shouldn't is a habit with authors.
It is a pity, of course, that looks should come into consideration at all. Yet this always has been an issue.
A Chicago reporter thought that Matthew Arnold resembled an elderly macaw picking at a trellis of grapes.
One New York reporter can testify that Arnold's way
of pronouncing the *a* in "handicraft" seemed funnier
than anything in his looks. However, looks are, if not
a liability, at least a responsibility. No speaker, for
example, should imperil attention to his early paragraphs by failing to be clearly visible for an appreciable
time before the call of the presiding person. Prospective listeners should be permitted to get through with
their astonishments. Thus I can remember that it appeared convenient to have Oscar Wilde sit on the lecture platform in full view, with his knee breeches and
silken hose, until the murmurs of comment upon the
physical facts had quite subsided.

However, it is not to be assumed that authors will
be outwardly odd. Eccentricity in clothes has never
been considered invalidating, for a man, and it is understood that, in the matter of clothes, men who can
keep unspotted from the world are more numerous
than in an earlier time, perhaps because women are
more ruthlessly vigilant or because dry cleaners are
more accessible. But in sheer disposition authors are,

as a class, worse than eccentric. They are concentric, while frequently giving the impression of having mislaid the common center.

Women authors, who have, in print, a peculiar facility in winning tenderness of response, are not less likely to rebuke high expectation. Aside from the annoyance which other women inevitably find in their clothes, women authors appear in person either as something that is called womanly, which seems, critically, to humanize if it does not belittle them, or they are obstreperous in some disenchanting way. It is assumed that women with the grand manner are obsolete, or it may be that the grand manner, as a spectacle, has begun to seem stodgy. Other manners, even when they escape the effect catty people call kittenish, have a precarious experience. An irritable woman is hard to adjust in any ritual of worship. An irritable man may have a tang. In a woman, acridity has a fatal flavor of loss, of a passed prime. There may be a technique to exasperation. In any case it is easier to fancy a peevish god than a goddess with a grouch. On the other hand, timid authoresses are, naturally, not impressive. If they have a new fame we now expect them to be noisy with it. If their fame is old they may slip into what might be called a second wistfulness, dazed as they are by current irreverence. This effect,

Meeting Authors

being strictly reminiscent, dissipates the attention of
the young and bruises the loyalty of the old. Celebrities must not be pathetic.

Having placed their private feelings on paper,
authors, we may fancy, have a tendency to be through
with them, so that being challenged, or seeming as on
the brink of being challenged, for more, comes hard.
They might like to be adored if the thing could be
made comfortable. An adorer who was equivalently
an artist might accomplish this apparent impossibility.
The truth is that real adorers fumble the crisis. Only
social magicians, to whom each obligation is strictly
objective, who have no conscience for anything but
the performance, are really successful. By such the
day is saved. Usually these have not read the book.
Reading the book takes time and may disturb the emotions. They have done better. They have read three
reviews, two of which discussed the ending, in
detail. Thus fortified against possibly glamourous influences they are fitted to handle the platitude that
meeting the author is meeting a situation. Being outraged by one of the criticisms, and being able to compare it with one less depraved, favors an easy conversational adventure.

One so skilled would know better than to tell an
author about the devastating disappointment of asking

for his book at the free library upon eight different occasions. The flattery of such persistence ought to have a beauty, and it can be beautiful so far as it goes. An author who did not feel the fame of a waiting list at the libraries would be blind to the finer implications. Yet his thought, however free of sordidness, would inevitably flit, perhaps only for an instant, as by the flashing flight of a mischievously winged question, toward imaginable bookstores, and this might tend to produce one of those absent-minded effects that are so detrimental to the flow of a perfect colloquy.

It would be absurd to suggest that all who meet authors are disposed to propitiate them. In a less enlightened era it may have happened that such meetings were looked to for dramatic qualities or at least for diversion of a refined sort. Before the days of radio and motion pictures when, among all possible amusements of a moral complexion, reading held a prominent place, even having fun with an author was imaginable. In any actually surviving interest there is, unquestionably, less of formula than before. Almost anything may happen. For one thing, the author may have talked on the radio, and it will be possible to tell him (or her) that every word was quite audible. Or his novel may have been filmed, which will give opportunity for comment on the outrageous liberties directors take. And the title; why on earth did they change the title? If he hasn't taken the "air," why has he remained aloof? Or doesn't he think that talking that way (if he hasn't done it) is rather *common?*

To speak of such detail is, however, an unpardonable digression, tempting as the little ironies may be. No writing person who is flippant about inadequate talk can occupy a graceful position. He might, indeed, help to illustrate the fact that writing persons *are* essentially disagreeable; whereas I am concerned in a more objective allusion to the peculiar peril of encounters against which the unsuspecting should be warned. Authors can do more than be vaguely unsatisfactory. Like Amy Lowell (with her appalling black cigar) they can be, socially, rather difficult to manage. They can be splendidly insulting, like Whistler, or they can offend by a mere word as Dickens did at the Boston dinner table when he alluded to some woman under discussion as looking "kissable," which was regarded not only as coarse but as just short of libidinous. They can, unless they are gravely traduced, reach heights and depths of offensiveness that make meeting them in the flesh an immoral risk. Only the specialist in the unpleasant can apprehend the whole story. No one, I think, has completed a proper anthology of ill-tempered authors, though much has been written, at one time or another, about individual frailties. In print these citations are always entertaining, or they are meant to be. The brutalities of a Hartmann or a Flaubert are recited as a pungence delightful in itself. The victims do not seem to matter. Moreover, they also are dead. Who will rebuke a chuckle over Doctor Johnson's savageries? Those that fell upon Boswell himself will make no one wince. Somehow we never feel realistically sorry for Boswell, which may be one of the proofs that Boswell was something of an artist. Certain other roughnesses of Johnson are more subject to humane anxiety. Yet the natural tendency is to give rough stuff news value. Sharp things make snappy reading.

Psychology might see "defensive" as a better word than "offensive" in estimating the acerbities of authors. It would be dishonest to permit the suspicion that authors can be outrageous without indicating that they often have imperative need to be so. If they are true to type and sensitive enough to be effective they are bound to carry a raw surface. It is wrong that an organism so easily hurt should tempt calamity by going about like tougher containers. If he needs to be upholstered against the chance of being bruised why does the artist venture forth?

Unfortunately for the success of a plea in behalf of

this infirmity, there are those social critics who find the chief trouble to be vanity. A Wagner who was a little surprised when, at a party, no woman fainted in awe of meeting him, is mentioned as a case in point; and of course there was Pope, "proud to see men, not afraid of God, afraid of me." Emerson (who complained of the "mountainous me" of Margaret Fuller) remarked that egotism is a kind of buckram that gives strength and concentration. "But," he added, "it spoils conversation."

Hazlitt, is of course, quite wrong when he says that no great man ever thought himself so. When Schopenhauer declared that he was the greatest philosopher of his time he was speaking with perfect moderation. What we call modesty is an artifice, a fruit of social repression. It is quite unlikely that any man is greater than he suspects. Self-realization is the backbone of genius.

Many years ago, in an important western hotel with an immense dining-room, I yielded my hat to a man who gave me a quick glance, gazed for a fraction of a second at the lining, then placed the hostage upon a certain shelf of a vast rack in which it appeared to be irretrievably obliterated. It would have seemed fantastic to imagine a necromancy by which that hat could ever be elicited from the impressive regimentation without the help of an owner's eye. Yet when I came again to the doorway fifty minutes or so later, my wizard, glancing again at my face, went without hesitation to the fourth section of the third shelf, peered for a verifying instant into the bowler, and handed to me my due.

It had the flavor of a miracle, and I said to the mute magician, "I suppose you are the greatest hat man in America."

"No," he said, without hesitation or modification of manner, "not the greatest. The greatest is at the Holland House, New York. I am the second greatest."

Who could withhold homage from so perfect a blend of self-respect and judicial-mindedness?

The reader may be left to translate this strictly historic incident into terms of another art. Fancy saying to an author—

But we can not fancy it. The impudence of the question—addressed to an author—is scarcely thinkable in a repressed world, yet a parallel to the beautiful retort might well illuminate a stretch of literary road.

Egotism may spoil conversation, but timidity makes worse havoc. And it would be a blunder not to see that sometimes it is the author who, out of his element, has the timidity, and the social inquisitor who has the cheek. Without citing the monstrous offenses of heavy-footed enemies, it is pertinent to indicate that many of the artist's personal antagonists commit subtleties of crime against peace.

The ability to meet authors rightly must, indeed, seem like a gift. One should say, offhand, that few have it, and that few who do have it can altogether escape misfortune. Nothing that requires special endowment should receive general encouragement. So that the warning must hold good; keep away from authors. A hero worshiper, above all others, should be an anchorite, if for no other reason than that revealed, in one of his early essays, by Max Beerbohm. It was, Beerbohm tells us, by the meeting of Walter Pater that he knew him to be vulnerable. If your chosen one misbehaves, even if he is not violently disagreeable, your hero is lost to you. If, by a miracle, he behaves handsomely, you are in the pitiful situation of finding that you have nothing left but a nice man.

The False Alternative

THE FALSE ALTERNATIVE

HE ASKED, with an innocent stupidity, Which do you prefer, blondes or brunettes? And I answered, quite seriously, that a wonderful philosophy, quickly available for any crisis, might be diagrammed upon the simple basis of his blunder.

The fact that his inquiry was open to a suspicion of flippancy did not affect the validity of my proposal. He may, indeed, have been utterly serious. Some men are deeply concerned about questions no more important than blondes or brunettes. His fatuity lay in assuming that he really had presented an alternative, or that I could be tricked. Of course, if I had not been habituated to the safeguard of this benevolent philosophy I might have fallen a victim. Ask a hundred people, Which do you prefer, Wagner or rag-time? summer or winter? city or country? At least eighty of them will not resent the affront. The mesmeric foolishness of the formula will influence an amazing number even of those who know enough to like both blondes and brunettes, both city and country, but who have escaped knowing that not only an uncomfortable

215

preference but a stultifying prejudice can be kindled by such inanities.

The trivial may here facilitate the significant. False alternatives are so common a cause of unhappiness, to the reformer and the wayfarer, to the student, the critic and the producer, that even the sillier assumptions, not in themselves to be dignified as false alternatives, come to a needless notice. We recognize in a phrase an unmistakable sign of that slavery to unnecessary choosing which can drive the enslaved into little habits of wabbling and thence to a cowering attitude before really necessary decisions. A habit of looking upon every pair of privileges as demanding a choice impoverishes the faculty for liking. A free initiative does not have to hate something to establish its liberty. It may love both. On the other hand it may hate both. To struggling minds it is often a fantastic relief to discover, with regard to a vast array of paired appearances and conditions that had seemed to say, Choose ye between us, that the challenge is fraudulent, that they can have both—or neither.

The struggling minds I am thinking of frequently give the effect of preferring the imposition. These minds know the words right and wrong, good and bad, correct and incorrect. They see life as made up of good people and bad people, of heroes and villains—

particularly of good women and bad women. The sky is blue and the grass is green. Their pictures must be painted that way. Green in the sky and blue in the leaves, like weaknesses in the hero or nobilities in the villain, are a bewilderment to people who hover over cheap alternatives. These are the people who believe that there are ten best novels, or a fixed set of greatest men. They are looking for authority, for imposed homage. They think there is a final way to pronounce a word as well as a definitive method of eating asparagus. They refuse to be enfranchised for the election that determines the fate of forms. Freedom to select or to reject is freedom to think, and thinking retains its old unpopularity. When one labor-saving dogmatist is upset, another is as welcome as a new fashion. What "they" say *now* is an imperative of subservience.

The abused "herd" is not to be marked as solely exemplifying the sin of shallow comparison. There are critics who do not feel that they have rightly extolled one writer unless they have backed their praise with disparagement of some other. They halt work upon the enthronement of a new idol to go and mutilate an old one. The new idol must be comparable to some other, and to make the point the quick means is to insult the archetype or the rival. If the new writer is by way of being a stylist what can be more effective in making readers understand than belittling De Quincey or Stevenson? That you should like both the new stylist *and* Stevenson, that you should warmly admire both *Jurgen* and *The Forest Lovers,* that you should delight in Pater and Birrell and Miss Repplier and Max Beerbohm and Huneker without repudiating Montaigne, is no more unreasonable than that you should, in finding contemporary satisfactions, respond joyously to both Mencken and Sherman. No new sea writer will ever induce me to throw an ink bottle at a portrait of Conrad, or of Herman Melville, and if a better than Dickens appears I shall not abase myself for having chuckled over Pickwick, nor waste any reader's time in an effort to drag him away from his new enthusiasm for confirmatory evidence.

Parenthetically, it is to be remarked that critics both lay and professional have a way of abusing a writer for rivaling himself. Individual preference seizes upon a book that may be a writer's first or his fifth, and all other work from the same hand is treated, by a certain sort of fanaticism, as an insolent pretense. Of course, the preference being individual, the attacks shift from book to book, which is an alleviation. This trait is closely related to the instinct that insists upon utter disparities, that is irked by the weighing of associated qualities, that despises a puzzling blend with-

out suspecting that of such are the unvarying plati-
tudes of nature.

The false alternative that approaches closer to the
true type is suggested by the literary prejudice against
neglect of defined forms. The alternative to conventional romance is not a realism that repudiates the romantic, but it seems to be necessary to the happiness of
the formalist that he should sit down before a shape
that accepts an orderly bi-party system. He wants no
split tickets. Above all he resents an attitude of mind
that ignores the dominating prominence of structural
grammar. The oddity is that they who have pio-
neered on the path to liberty, or who set up as having
done so, are often most schoolmasterish toward of-
fenders against newly reached conclusions. Such
monitors leave a theater in a state of chagrin because,
three-quarters of the way through, an admirable performance was suddenly poisoned by a device that made
the whole thing not a good *play*. The audience may
have liked the offense more than anything else in the
show, but this is remarked as emphasizing the evil.
No form of art is more intensively ritualized than a
stage play, which may account for the circumstance
that the only escape that accomplishes relief is that
through mechanically permitted but troublesome obscenity.

The False Alternative

In the matter of theoretical indecency we may sympathize with Havelock Ellis, who carefully considered the aesthetics of obscenity and concluded that one may approve obscenity in principle yet find that "in practice even its recognized masters barely attain success." Small, loose, undisciplined men, according to Ellis, never can be "rightly obscene." "It is that touch that stamps their genius. It gives profundity and truth to their vision of life." Thus there must be an obverse to a reverse. There must be a stage setting for what Lucretius called the *postcenia vitae,* and no easy obviousness of dividing line between the "decent" and the "indecent" can authenticate the false alternatives of stupid analysis.

The alternative to *this* is *that*—thus runs the decree. After me, the deluge. The alternative to a quarrelsome marriage is not more control and concession, but divorce. What may be the real alternative (one must abide the testimony) can be called a quibble. An alternative to a repressed childhood is recklessly indicated as a childhood without experience in meeting plain social imperatives or without the guidance of ideals. A psychology that pleads for a liberated initiative is pointed out (by those who take the trouble) as outlawing obligation, as if, in the art of living, orchestration were abandoned in the interest of wholly

individualistic tootings. The real alternative is not a
new form but a new feeling, not another set of rules
but another individual sense of relationship. The child
is now a person, but it is a related person. In escaping
repressions it does not escape accountability, which
must mean that we ask from it more and not less than
we asked before. Poor child! Grudgingly released
from the old restraints, bitterly challenged to make
good—to be wisely young, to be gracefully kept. Poor
parents! Asked to abandon domination yet to be the
providing philosophers and friends—to be gods who
never break the wings of free will.

Youth is jostled by a thousand false alternatives
that seek to bar cards, theaters, dancing, dress liberties,
and what-not. Social fundamentalism sternly points
out that the alternative to established restriction is hell.
Sin's statutes are revised, but hell remains as the other
prong of the choice. Civilization, meanwhile, keeps
its cheerfulness before prophecies of disaster by the
excitement of finding that most of the forecasts are
constructed upon false data.

National prohibition (I demand room for a few
solemnities) was based upon a false alternative. Real
temperance—volitional mastery in the presence of
privilege—was making extraordinary strides in America when the calamity fell. The safeguarding of weak-

ness and the control of ugly abuses had a long way to go, but they were on their way. While the progress of decency was slow it moved with integrity. Its triumphs were without shame. These were deduced from the common experience of mankind. If there was general recognition of the need for greater haste the alternative to the old order was not a legislative subterfuge but a quickening of the movement toward temperance—toward the real alternative, with the legislative cooperation that could be backed by genuine sentiment. Hurry has done worse than obscure the goal. It has produced the country's greatest scandal, its most shocking disorganization of ideals. It can not permanently retard the natural evolution of decency, yet it has made necessary a bitter travail by which the country may be a long time in coming again to a sure-footed advance.

Politicians delighted, at one time, in false alternatives as to the enfranchisement of women. When they had elaborated all the drivel about woman's sphere and the disasters that only awaited her attention to the ballot box (as if voting took a month), they pointed apprehensively to the polling place. I can remember certain city polling places which voters approached with ballots held in bunches by elastic bands. The voting line sometimes extended for several hundred feet, per-

The False Alternative

haps in the rain, under the surveillance of heelers who were able to know that a watched sheaf of ballots went duly to the boxes. At sundown it was not uncommon to see the door close on a long line of would-be voters, shut out, perhaps, by the use of interjected repeaters. The atmosphere of a polling place was indeed sadly unsavory. With a gesture of stalwart solicitude the politician (and his abetters) could bellow: "Shall our wives and daughters be subjected to *this?*" The simple multiplication of polling places and the cleaning up of the entire system quite spoiled the politician's picture. Yet his stupid theories of alternative delayed an amiable amendment to the constitution.

Labor and business have floundered among false alternatives, always with the likelihood that "human nature" would be cited to imply anything that was needful to facilitate a blundering theory. Russia found the answer to one despotism in another despotism. The irony was not the fruit of any logic so symmetrical, but the quoted philosophy offers a good enough illustration of the false alternative. You must, says the cynicism of Marx, either ride or be ridden. As always, any true alternative is called a compromise, if not something worse. The search of the fanatic is for the most violent antithesis rather than for the truth. A fanatic patriotism reaches the peak of the absurdity.

The False Alternative

Every war writes the false alternative on its banners.

Thus with attacks upon a failed church. A moron or hypocrite in a pulpit is a temptation to fantastic conclusions. Colleges are asked to decide as between athletics and scholarship, or between standardized scholarship and individualism, as if such fixed alternatives really existed. The teacher is asked to decide as between his individual instincts and the demands of his office, as if any who serve the mass might survive the actual application of such a choice. The grotesque logic generally is applied to the other fellow's trade.

The wasting friction of false alternatives is the more to be resented since true alternatives are always with us. The true crisis is a sufficient tax on wisdom and courage, or on the sense of humor. Seeing it as it is begins our test. On the one hand is the need to stay alive and honest. On the other is the true alternative—like that which says that preaching *must* stop short of boredom.

The Hush

THE HUSH

It is an awkward thing to have entered an era in which we are asked to reform and to be natural at the same time. Men have come through bursts of naturalness, and they have not seemed to be permanently injured by paroxsyms of reformation, but to be concurrently free and refined, for instance, must always appear complicated. Passionate appeals for spontaneity stir us to do our bit. There is no longer any argument against the awfulness of a repression. Yet other considerations call us. The awkwardness must be plain even to enthusiastic crusaders against noise.

Fancy the din of a neolithic dinner! In that splendid tumult, punctuated by magnificent crunchings, and giving space and privilege to the chorused gusto of rude appetites, man must have made mighty sounds. A spectator who could for the moment have forgotten the raw beauty of the scene might have found in the symphonic uproar a truer revelation of Man than is encompassed by all the later fumblings of psychology. An ear rightly attuned would have deduced from a study of the Knights, at a time when they were throwing denuded bones under the Round Table, a better understanding than was possible to any sentimental Tennyson. It is probable that eating silently has resulted in spiritual stultifications of a far-reaching sort. The prophets of old who dipped their crusts into the common tureen could be simple men. They were not stultified by futile concessions. No taboo had yet vulgarized the primal music of mastication. Their whole-hearted eating must have helped to establish that gastric integrity which centuries of politeness have not wholly succeeded in breaking down.

Without the testimony of children we are able to learn that noise is a naturalness. The instinct to enjoy the sound of our own processes is, indeed, repeatedly indicated as incident to our habit-longing for expression. The blacksmith's joyous supplement to the strictly necessary blows of his weapon is a beautiful case in point. As the grandson of a blacksmith, who has heard what he has heard, I speak with a precise authority. John MacCrae was as good a blacksmith as he was a preacher, and his gifts blended at the forge, for not only did he raise his voice in song, but he appreciated those noble melodies of the anvil liberated by complementary strokes of the hammer, strokes long ago orchestrated with splendid effect. Not to know the concertos of a blacksmith's shop, not to have appre-

The Hush

hended the sublime clangor that rises beside a bidden flame, is to miss a proper dream of what it was the divine blacksmith made for Siegfried, not rightly to surmise why the Sword of the Spirit was called the Word of God.

It would be absurd to pretend that all occupational sounds hold an equivalent glory, but I am assured that the carpenter not only knows but needs the cry of the driven nail and that sibilant shriek of his own jack-plane. If you understand carpentering you understand its impacts. The technique of nailing is capable of exquisite refinements. These are welcome to the educated ear. Because I do not understand the steam riveter, the piercing thunder of the steam riveter seems to me the most hellish of all contemporary sounds. Yet to the riveter, the crescendo is unquestionably a real nourishment.

Every occupation advertises some phase of the same instinct. The man up-stairs does not feel that his shoes are off until he has made the floor understand. When some one six flights up shoots himself, the thing passes without notice upon the theory, mentioned by the janitor at the inquest, of a slammed door. The natural way to know that a door is closed, as any child may teach us, is by the detonation. Some people can look for a cravat or a glove in various drawers of a dresser upon the same theory. Each thud seems to say (with a particular malice when the apartments are sound-proof), "Well, it isn't in *that* drawer, anyway," unless the searcher is a fragile lady imperfectly addicted to swearing, in which case the thud can be not only what an earlier observer called a wooden damn, but can have a rich obscenity with a gamut of inflections.

It may turn out that silence is a degenerate ideal. Some of the noisiest books we have are written in praise of silence. When we say that a man likes to hear himself talk, we are uttering the veriest platitude. One's own bronchial reliefs are the true basis of vocal art. It is so with all expression. Perhaps you have never seen a girl typist weeping over a new-fangled silent machine. How can you feel busy if you are noiseless? How can you be brisk on rubber heels? Imagine a man at a trolley lever who could not get an answering thunder. Imagine a restaurant dish washer after a well-meaning science has invented rubber plates!

Hence the bus boy before they have tamed him. The strictly natural waiter likes to hear his own efficiency, to get the *pianissimo* and then the proper *forte* of an unfolding effect. Subdued by refinements he is never again the same man. In cushioned arenas you

The Hush

see but the wraiths of a species intended to startle the ear, pitiful ghosts of a departed health.

However, it is in domestic noises that we get the sharpest suggestion of dangerous ideals. Natural husbands upset esthetic systems that are a shade too delicate. Innocent as it may look, a toothpick has repeatedly destroyed a perfectly good marriage. The "extreme cruelties" of many a divorce document are legal afterthoughts abetted by the inventiveness of woman. The real trouble was nasal. Rather handsome cave-man snores have resulted in more separations than the silentest drinkings. When love was simpler and strong men were strong men, there was no debate over the trivial rhythms of life. In those days men ate soup in a manly way. They had virile, bearded appreciations. Silent maleness is modern, but it may lead, one must fear, to deep depravities.

Thus all noisy offenses are subject to quick identification. We know where they are. It may be well that societies for the abatement of noise should give serious thought to the risks of too promiscuous campaigns. Nature is a liberal, now majestically silent, now roaring superbly. The universe is run under a long-time contract. It will not do to be too reckless with mufflers. The Great Terror may be Silence.

Le Quartier

LE QUARTIER

THE two original Latin Quarters, the one of Paris
and the pleasant echo in New York, have long since
gone, both with rumbles of lament. There was good
reason why I should most bewail the passing of the
New York version. This was a more delicate, as well
as a more tentative expression of art life, and I knew
it better. Doubtless a feeling about the New York
Quarter was influenced to the end by the earlier
glimpse of Paris, brief as that had been.

To be nineteen and to be in Paris for the first
time—it was, at the entering moment, like stepping into
the vestibule of romance. An enormous magic seemed
to impend. Charts of travel diagrammed the haunts of
significant ghosts. Balzac, Flaubert, Hugo, the de
Goncourts and the rest had woven the spell, had placed
subtle marks upon the scene lying open to the sentimental prowler. How droll and how impressive are
the illusions kindled by art!—the triteness of the young
emotion is repeated, I have no doubt, in this mention
of it. Yet art will die when such spells fail. I can
smile but I do not regret in recalling the young pilgrim

235

who scurried across the Pont Neuf to cast himself into the Quartier.

The concierge at 56 Rue de St. Andrè des Arts said that there was a room. In any place of an Exposition there was always a chance that there would not be a room. I was reassured, and followed the energetic little man with the fluffy black mustache up the winding stone steps, which were to have lamp light on each second landing. The fourth floor front room had the effect of being two, for the bed was within a partitioned space. A Swiss clock stood under a glass case on the mantel. There were a table, two chairs and a wall book-rack. Best of all was the French window with a tiny balcony opening upon the faint alluring clatter of the street. I was enchanted. Having undertaken to tramp through Europe (at a total cost of one hundred and eighty-five dollars, including steerage fares) this waxed and gracious eyrie was a sort of dissonance. I saw it as a reprehensible splendor. But it was in the Quarter. One might be briefly extravagant in the Quarter. Had I not saved ardently by sleeping in newsboys' lodging-houses . . . ?

The rate, said the concierge, would be five francs. A lot of money. Five—I counted them out to the little man with the fluffy mustache, feeling guilty and elated. The shiny floor and the clock and the French

window bade me abandon myself. I unpacked the
black bag and put the guide book and journals in the
book-rack. Already I began to feel like an established
resident. Beyond the sill of that window was Paris.
There was the throb as of a great pulse. . . .

I had seen a little restaurant a few doors
away. . . . A first dinner—or say a supper cheap
enough to begin atonement for the reckless five francs.
The restaurant recalled the Bowery, which it should
not have done. It was a narrow slab of a place. Viands
were described in script labels on the walls. The writer
of these had been impulsive. I could read nothing.
But I had been plugging at French for months. A
cheap supper required few words. The one waiter
hovered and saluted me. What would I? By way of
a practise spin in the vernacular—it would have seemed
perfunctory and not rightly in the neighbor manner to
start talking about food—I asked, "At what hour does
the Exposition open in the morning?"

"*Oui, M'sieur!*" he ejaculated, without an instant's
hesitation, and was off. I stared after him as he
bawled into the recesses at the back. And presently
he brought me a large dish and three subsidiary dishes.
They were thrillingly good to eat. I never knew what
they were. I only knew that I had described them ex-
plicitly when I asked at what hour the exposition

opened in the morning. If I had been less hungry I
might have been more chagrined. It was plain that my
French must be worse than anything I had suspected.
Fortunately the misadventure cost me no more than
an even franc. I might have been ruined.

Later in the evening I had another encounter with
the language—and a Person. There had come a tap
at my door. After the event I recognized it as an in-
sinuating tap—a mere whisper of a true knock. Being
partly undressed I blew out the lamp before turning
the knob. . . .

A young woman. At first she was not very clear,
since my floor belonged to the alternately dim series
of stair landings. She had to be ascertained by the
lamp of the floor below and the lamp of the floor
above. But while she spoke I became aware that she
was pleasant to look upon. And I did not understand
her. In view of her errand it was outrageous that I
should ask her to say it again. Then I understood.
The concierge had told her that there was a new young
man who was alone. Was it possible that the new
young man, at present, perhaps, unacquainted with the
Quarter, might like a companion who would attend to
all the little affairs of living and—

No—I thanked her fearfully. I tried (with the
door space narrowed to the width of my head) to tell

her that the concierge was very kind and that she was
very kind but that really I had a way of being alone—.
I suppose she understood as few words as the waiter
had, but unlike him (being aided by the door gesture)
she got the drift. And she thanked me as sweetly as if
I had told her to go and fetch her trunk.

Perhaps I was somewhat jumpy when the other
knock came after my breakfast the next morning. This
time it was the concierge, who astounded me by re-
fusing a word. He simply beckoned. I was to follow
him. On the floor below, in a room corresponding to
mine, a middle-aged English artist, with silver rimmed
spectacles, was at work, close to the window, upon a
sweetish water color.

I gathered some of the truth when the concierge
began his quick speech to the painter. The rest soon
appeared.

"The concierge says," the Englishman remarked,
rattling a brush in a glass of water, "that your rent is
five francs a day, and will you please pay every morning?"

"*A day!*" I thanked the artist. I thanked and
paid the rent-gatherer and tottered up-stairs to the
shiny room that had seemed to be five francs a week.
I had said "week"—distinctly—when I asked the rent.
It would have been insulting to speak more meticulous-

ly. Five francs *a day!* This meant that if I stayed
five days I could get no further into Italy than Milan.
If I stayed ten days I should be halted (financially) at
Geneva. After all, I did have eight days *and* Milan,
but I had very little to eat on the way back to Liver-
pool and the ship. The truth was (as some research
showed) that prices were up for the Exposition
time—and no later Paris exposition has ever seen them
go down again.

Thus I came to the greatest extravagance of my
tramping trip and to the happy delirium of the Quarter. I had never tasted wine, but I could buy coffee
at the Café Procope, soon to close its historic doors,
and fancy that Voltaire had written upon the very table
at which I sat. It was an American boy (he thought
me a freak, even after I told him about the one hundred and eighty-five dollars and how little was left)
who took me into a few of the studios, to the glittering
Jardin Mabile, and the Bal Boullier. The spectacle of
a youthful New Yorker who had no pipe and who
would not taste the *ordinaire* may have been worth his
trouble. One counts up his Good Samaritans with
what may be a complacence, yet with a kindled complacence. Perhaps, by the grace of God, *we* are
counted in some other list.

The Latin Quarter to be ascertained in later days

had undergone the obliterations so poetically and so dramatically mourned by many a Parisian writer as well as by many an American. New York's echo of *Le Quartier* was of that earlier phase. You found it where you now find a modernized Greenwich Village. I began to know it well after returning from that first acquaintance with the Pont Neuf, to know how it straggled, and how it was much more a spirit than a region. In the Café de Paris, on the southeast of Washington Square, where Monsieur wore a skullcap and talked to the parrot in the window, and where Madame, with her round florid face, did all the hard work, I used to see artists from the Benedick and the West Tenth Street Studios—Chase, La Farge, Blum, Quartley, Robert W. Chambers while he was still a painter and had yet to write *The King in Yellow*, Cassilear, de Haas, "Bootblack" Brown, and the writing men such as Stockton, Howells, Gilder, Bunner, Charles de Kay and Thomas Janvier. Janvier celebrated a restaurant in a street or two above the square as the "Café Napoleon." The Café de Paris, like the original Black Cat, came to be much written, and its doom was sealed, for it moved up into University Place, hired waiters, lost its flavor and was gone. The Tile Club understood the Quarter. *Scribner's* illuminated its haunts. Artist attics, whose masters knew

241

Le Quartier

Paris *when,* could not but be colored by gaieties in the
Quartier manner. Such picturesqueness was provocative to writing talent, and attention from the magazines and newspapers undermined the innocence of
Eden. Moreover it crowded the alleys. The Quarter
became self-conscious. Landlords had yet to learn that
if they painted the door a bright green they could double the rent, but landlords themselves managed to become artists—commercial artists. For a considerable
period, while the 'nineties waned and the new century
came in, the Square had a strongly literary flavor,
while the French Quarter extended northward. It was
not until the time of the Great War that the Village
was accused of becoming bizarre. The last vestiges of
the old Latin Quarter traditions had been brushed away.

Each Youth has its Quarter, its *true* Bohemia. The
era before is marked as musty. The era after is called
sordid if not degenerate. Physical changes are ever
a brutality to some one. Old artists know the geo-
graphical as well as the spiritual boundaries of the
Golden Age, and they like to warn the new school that
it too will presently be old stuff. Then a fame may
get its "second wind," though this may be after the
old have gone. Thus Pfaff's on Broadway, with its
stories of Poe, Walt Whitman, Fitz-James O'Brien
and John Wilkes Booth, comes again under the spot-

light. We make literary paragraphs over the controversy as to just where Pfaff's stood, as Paris may quarrel over the Procope. "The Pfaff crowd" was irritating or congenial as (say) the Algonquin crowd is to-day. The landmark or the region or the state of mind that has just died is deader than it ever will be again, though this can be no consolation to the freshly bereaved. Thus it is with men and movements. A displaced fashion becomes first a joke. It is yet to have its day in court—the court of history. The man who is outmoded shares the first fate of the giants. The second fate rests upon chances outside the domain of fashion.

The Happy Ending

THE HAPPY ENDING

CRITICS often seem to hover over a work of written art with a cynical impatience for the finish. No enthusiast at a ringside ever screamed more truculently for the knockout. To these, March, however it may have come in, must go out like a lion. Intervening performances are negligible. It is true that many a house visitor ruins his reputation by not knowing how to go home. I don't mean merely *when* to go home. The art here is not in mere duration. Many an excessively long call has been glorified by a master-stroke of departure. So with a speech. We all have heard speakers who have spent their whole time in fumbling for a way to sit down. Tradition crippled them from the moment they stood up. We may fancy a skeptical critic, jostled by an uproar of approval for eloquence, muttering, "Yes, but *watch how he ends!*"

Efficiency has a formula: Never make a speech unless you have an ending with you. Just how far such a prescription may apply to the art of fiction, for example, continues to be a matter of acidulous debate. We have discarded the ancient mold, and there will be no peace until something equally stabilizing has been hammered into final shape. The ancient mold, fixed in the youth of story-telling, implied that tales however fantastic or heart-breaking must end happily. The story-teller was released by a consciousness of his terminating privilege. He could wring hearts (and necks) with a free hand and never suffer from a repression, since his one trivial obligation was easily met when the time came. The reader was able to abandon himself in the same spirit. He knew that after all his agonies he was likely to understand that the dead were better dead, and that somebody was to be left in a situation of tranquil if not ecstatic comfort.

This common expectation had two conspicuous results. The truckler began to accentuate his sop, to make it soppier, to cultivate a tenderness toward all expectation. The rebel, resenting formulas, and influenced on occasion by the joy of ástonishing, if not by a religious antipathy to tradition, set about the business of defeating the calculated curve. If this could not be accomplished by a crescendo of misery he would not end at all. He would simply stop. When realism came in, life was indicated as supporting all rebellion. Life seldom ended happily. Neither could mere frustration be standardized. Existence might not end with an ironic question. Most frequently the interruption was of a dropped curtain.

The Happy Ending

There were readers to support any accentuated system. They flocked to the sentimentalist. They coddled the rebel. They wanted things the same and they wanted them different. The artist found himself by no means single-minded in the matter. Sometimes the logic of inevitableness led him straight to a piece of beauty. Again it led straight into an ugly impasse. The conservative says that human nature is as it is. The liberal says, but human nature grows: let us encourage the growth. The radical, who is a liberal in a hurry, says, let us begin now by smashing tradition. Tradition so often needs to be smashed, all progress holds so lively an implication of obliterated habit, that art is frequently halted in dismay. Unfortunately for the extreme view the sense of beauty is essentially a sense of tradition—that is to say, a sense of association. Thus we can not smash *all* tradition. To escape the vacuum we must have something just as good. Evidently the quick or the gradual training of readers must always be an obligation of art. Meanwhile the great audience will ever be a disappointment. People who hate to think, and who care to feel only when it comes easy, will inevitably compose that majority to which the artist may yield a wistful stare.

At the moment there is one sort of ending which the sensitive artist must regard with apprehension. A tale may end cheerfully or it may end tragically but it must not end with a marriage. We all have known marriages that were not an ending, that were in fact only a dreadful beginning. But "and so they were married" connotes the sentimental. It does not matter that the characters thus are led to the mouth of a pit. If they marry at the end of the book the beans are spilled. To risk the personal, I know one novel adjudged by a distinguished (and kindly) critic as escaping genuine bigness by the misfortune of a happy ending—namely, by a marriage. Another able critic lamented, of the same book, that it ended with so savage a piece of irony! It was marriage that made the trouble. Any other cheerfulness or any other sarcasm would have eluded the qualifying word. If two men, after various business adventures, had struck up a precarious partnership, the imagination would not have been snubbed. Statistics would have kept us from figuring an inevitably happy ending for them. But a business partnership does not carry a flabby connotation. It may be perilous but it is not mushy.

If an alert esthetic censorship should succeed in keeping artists away from any but disastrous marriages—introduced early enough to reveal the essential details of the disaster—ingenuity would not be bereft. People do more than marry, and if profuse suspense could precede rescue by way of a trite marriage, equivalent complexity may follow one that is to furnish the sinister note. We do not have duels any more, but the automobile has brought back the bandit, the airplane guarantees a rich field of adventure in elopement or beauty-snatching, easy divorce multiplies opportunities once sparingly provided to comedy or tragedy, and the nervous intricacy of modern life otherwise furnishes raw material enough even for high pressure production in plots. No matter what may be done about endings, invention will find its feet. When putting the end at the beginning has been long obsolete, when every sophisticated plot contains an early assurance that nobody marries—at least not legally—when sex strategies of pursuit are used not as a convention to provide suspense but to furnish incidental humor or to carry cross lights on character, there will remain for analysis and for surprise a vast area of introverted emotions. We will never be through with sex until we are through with life, yet it is absurdly true that fiction lags far behind other arts in candidly recognizing vital prominences of human movement.

What fiction may do at last about diagrams that lead to marriage is, after all, of much less importance than the living implications reflected in the prejudice. If marriage itself is to be a bathos we shall have to begin revising our social technique, for even a cynicism that waives surprise looks, however apathetically, for ways to make life interesting. The antiquity of boredom is not a fresh discovery. Perhaps all that is happening is simply another outburst of resentment against natural conditions that insist on staying put. The outburst has new terms. New indignations must, to be effective, have some novelty. That marriage does so little to change marriers is no more outrageous than that art should do so little to change its spectators. And we must remember that complaining about art is a great deal less inculpating than complaining about life. The wretched result of insisting upon realism is that we lose a happy ease of escape. If the ancient art theory of the happy ending is forever repudiated, and if we are to have no better company than an accusatory realism, do we incur a need to give up, for our embodied selves, a perhaps sheepish wish to end happily? Beauty antedates books, but the sense of beauty is coeval with art, and we must expect to find in one field a hint of what is happening and what will happen in the other.

To put it bluntly, must we serve consistency by keeping away from marriage in life itself? Or, if we do marry, must we see to it that the arrangement does not proceed happily? Will a sense of futility, of hav-

The Happy Ending

ing incurred exasperation, cloud the closing chapter of a life that was entertainingly turbulent, that was, it may be, properly punctuated with the reprehensible, but that threatens to close with an absurd peace?

There would be a huge difficulty in fitting life to its proper art. One might save up a "stinger" for the end and loosen it too soon. A man may know the page upon which he is to finish a book yet fail at measuring his own final paragraphs of breath. Who does not know of a witty death-bed deviltry that went flat because of a ludicrously anticipated cue? No ingenuity can provide against a blunder in the ringing down of the curtain, against a tranquil pause that would amount to an esthetic blight on a well calculated career. As by the code of a speech maker or a satisfactory novelist, one should, indeed, know how to fade like an artist, with at least one credible witness who would be in a position to proclaim that he refused the tawdry temptation to end happily.

THE END